ELVAN GEORGE

Athletic Director and Head Football Coach, Ada, Oklahoma, High School

The Split-T in

High School Football

Englewood Cliffs, N.J.

PRENTICE-HALL, INC., 1958

83547

Foreword

In *The Split-T in High School Football,* Elvan George has made a clear-cut, concise, easily understood explanation of the theory of the Split-T attack.

In addition, he has made a careful analysis and explanation of the methods he has used so successfully in teaching this style of play.

The Split-T in High School Football should be of great interest not only to Split-T coaches, but to all people interested in the great game of football.

CHARLES "BUD" WILKINSON
Head Football Coach
University of Oklahoma

The Adaptation of the Split-T to High School Football

My SUBJECT IS NOT TO INTRODUCE A NEW football offense or to reveal the mysteries of the Split-T offense. Instead, this book applies to the high school coach the theories and objectives that are already in use by colleges and universities.

We shall affirm these propositions:

1. A high school coach can effectively apply the Split-T offense as taught in universities and colleges to his team.
2. The high school coach will be able to operate successfully using only the four basic running plays and the four basic pass plays as his entire offense.
3. A high school team can handle the difficult option play, which is the risky problem-maker that causes many high school coaches to seek other means of running wide.
4. The exacting performance required for the Split-T can be taught in the short practice time available to most high school coaches.

The basic running plays for the Split-T will be listed as: the Halfback Hand-off, the Fullback Counter, the Fullback Slant and the Option. These plays may be run to each side with identical maneuvers. The basic passes are: the Counter Pass, the Slant Pass, the Option Pass and the Swing or Reverse Pass.

These plays will be our basic offense. We shall, however, include a chapter on special or related plays, plays that are often used in conjunction with the Split-T for the purpose of upsetting the defense mentally, and which thereby help to make the regular attack move more effectively when the team returns to it.

Realizing that one of the chief factors confronting all high school coaches is the lack of time, we are submitting a plan for complete organization, including use of mechanical and visual aids, as well as a timed practice schedule.

E. G.

Table of Contents

The Theory of the
Split-T Offense

SINCE THE SPLIT-T OFFENSE HAS BEEN used by college coaches so successfully and is currently a very popular formation in high school, the theory of the Split-T is well established. It is my opinion that adapting the Split-T theory to high school football requires very little change and it is my intention to transpose the accepted theory with little revision.

The Split-T formation is designed to exploit to the fullest the advantages the rules give to the offensive team. The rules favor the offense over the defense in that the offensive team knows when the ball will be snapped. The offense knows what the play will be and has the advantage of always being in favorable field position because the ball is played off the hashmarks, which are 18 yards from the sidelines. These advantages must be exploited fully in our high school version.

The quick, straight-ahead thrust of the Split-T exploits the advantage of knowing when the ball will be snapped. The offensive lineman is coiled for the straight-forward drive into his opponent, and the block is exploded on the count to hit the defender suddenly and unexpectedly. The Split-T ball-carrier's eyes are on the line ahead and he can race past the defensive lineman before he has time to recover. Since the Split-T lineman is not required to pull out of the line, he may have his weight forward, enabling him to hit quickly on the snap in his normal, straight-ahead manner. The backfield man is not required to take the ball from the quarterback, but the quarterback has the responsibility of placing the ball in a pocket formed by the ball-carrier's hands as he breaks into the line with utmost speed. No other offense uses more effectively the advantage of knowing when the ball will be snapped than the Split-T.

Since the line is balanced and the backfield is the Straight-T, the Split-T exploits the advantage of knowing what the play will be.

The perfect balance of the offense compels the defense to protect against a play that may hit equally well in any direction. Flankers are infrequently used; and in the basic attack (which is our concern in this book) they are not used at all. An offense that shows more power in one direction before the ball is snapped is not using completely the advantage of knowing what the play will be. The balanced striking power of the Split-T conceals more favorably the point of attack.

The offensive advantage of having the ball in favorable field position at the hashmarks is extended by the Split-T's potential to either side of the line. All basic plays are identical when run to the right or left, so when faced with a defense that is wide-field conscious, the Split-T may run all basic plays effectively from the hashmarks into the sideline.

Maintaining Possession of the Ball

By exploiting these advantages to the fullest, the Split-T enables the offense to maintain possession of the ball. The key to winning football is to *maintain possession of the ball,* since obviously our opponents can't score while we have the ball. It follows that the team that has the ball for the majority of the game reduces the time that they must play defense, and thereby has a better chance of winning.

One of the first problems for the coach in applying the principles of the Split-T to high school football is to teach the players, and particularly the quarterback, that the sole purpose of the offense is to make *first down.* Many offensive players think only of making the long gain. Although this is an admirable objective, it is an unrealistic approach. When faced with good opposition, it will be difficult to gain yardage and virtually impossible to make a long gain every play. However, by observing the principles of the Split-T, consistent short gains will result.

The short gains will produce the first downs that will enable the offense to maintain possession of the ball, and a series of first downs will eventually score.

Obviously a four yard gain is a tremendously successful play. In any field position, three consecutive 4-yard gains will get a first down. The Split-T team must realize that a 4-yard play is a great play. The plays of the Split-T are designed consistently to produce a 4-yard gain.

Avoid a Poor Call

With the 4-yard play as prime objective, it is apparent that an equally potent factor is that the offense must not make a poor call. A poor call is a play that fails to gain—or loses—yardage, since one such play in any series of downs would be likely to stop the offense, forcing it to give up the ball. For this reason the strategy of the Split-T will be to try to avoid the poor call even more than trying to call a long-gaining play.

To sum up the theory of the Split-T offense as it has been handed down to the high school teams by the college coaches: The high school quarterback must primarily be concerned with avoiding the poor call. Having done that effectively, a 4-yard gain per play should be realized, with three such plays netting the offense a first down. A consecutive series of first downs results in a score, and allows the team to maintain possession of the ball. Consistent short gains will consume a great deal of time and cut down the time that the team will have to play defense.

With the objective of the Split-T established, the high school coach's next move is to specify the principles of the offense that will enable his team to accomplish the objective:

1. The offense must hit with all possible speed. Since

the Split-T quarterback shuttles up and down the line, it is imperative that the offensive lineman must explode out of his stance and engage the defender on the defensive side of the line of scrimmage. Even with a good blocker doing his task well, a strong defensive lineman cannot be contained for long. Therefore, the Split-T ball-carrier must race past the defensive man while he is still involved with the blocker. A stance must be taught to both halfbacks and all linemen that will enable them to move straight ahead at their greatest speed. Since every basic move of the fullback and quarterback starts them parallel to the line of scrimmage, they should have stances that permit them to move laterally in the best possible manner. *Speed* is the most important single fundamental of the Split-T in high school.

2. The offense must hit with speed over a broad front. It is much easier for the defense to defend a narrow front than a broad one, so the line splits to spread the defense. A point for the high school player to learn thoroughly is that the offense splits the line to spread the defense. Many offensive linemen think of splitting to obtain a blocking angle, which experience has taught us will lead to most unfavorable results. Most defensive linemen have been assigned to play directly in front of some portion of the offensive player's body, such as his outside shoulder. If the offensive lineman attempts to split for a blocking angle on a defender with this assignment, the lineman will find that he is actually closing the hole he wanted to open. If the offensive lineman will think of spreading the defense in this situation, the de-

fender will move with him to head up with the outside shoulder, and an opening will be created in the defensive line through which the offense has a better chance to gain. However, if the defensive man has been assigned to play a certain distance from his teammate and will not move with splitting lineman, a blocking angle will result. By properly splitting, the offense can force the defense into an unfavorable position.

3. The offensive team must fake well. By faking well the offensive players keep the defense in doubt as to where the play will be run. The basic maneuver of the Split-T attack is the quick straight-ahead thrust. This powerful drive straight into the line puts a great deal of pressure on the defense. Therefore, to realize the full potential of the offense, all of the wide plays and passes must start with the fake of this straight-ahead thrust. The linemen must fire out on wide plays and passes exactly as they do on the inside play or the defense will not be confused. The back, hitting in, carries his fake through and runs exactly as if he had the ball. The defense is thus forced to hold its position and defend against the possibility of the fast inside play. The delay brought about by good faking will prevent the defense from recovering to the outside quickly enough to stop the wide plays, and the defensive secondary will be in poor position to cover well should the running pass develop.

Summary

The theory of the Split-T may be summed up by say-ing that the best way to reach our objective (which is to make first down) is to hit with all possible speed over a broad front. This is created by splitting the line, with good inside faking at all times. In order for these principles to be carried out effectively in high school, certain fundamentals must be taught thoroughly with a great amount of attention to detail. These fundamentals include: *proper stance; lining up on the ball; splitting properly; getting off on the count;* and *faking well.* The player's stance is designed to enable him to move as fast as possible. Lining up on the ball properly gives us a chance to outcharge our opponents. All of the plays will start with the same maneuver, and with a good inside fake the defense will be confused.

Trap plays, which work so well in other offenses, are not so effective with the Split-T, since the linemen have so much weight forward that they are handicapped in pulling out of the line for the trapping assignment. Since the Split-T quarterback steps up into the line as he receives the ball from the center, he will be slow and awkward on drop-back passes. These and other attractive features of other formations do not lend themselves readily to the Split-T. It is not my intention to say that the high school Split-T coach is unable to use plays from other formations, but merely that the basic Split-T offense is most effective when used alone.

Teaching Split-T Fundamentals to High School Athletes

THE FIRST FUNDAMENTAL WE WILL DIS-
cuss is the stance of the players in the Split-T Offense.
The stance is well established and is adapted to an
offense that requires him to move forward quickly. Only
the quarterback and fullback have a normal pattern of
movement that requires them to move laterally, so both
halfbacks and all of the linemen have their weight forward, ready to move straight ahead at top speed. Since
we are not advocating any change from the accepted
stance of the Split-T linemen and backs, we will present
only a short description of the stance, and then move
on to the best methods of teaching the high school player
to take his stance properly.

The Lineman's Stance

The lineman's feet should be split the width of his
shoulders. He should drop neither toe back farther than

the heel of the other foot. His back must be straight and his head must be up. The buttocks are carried high since the emphasis is on speed and we do not want to have to raise the buttocks before starting forward. Our lineman places considerable weight on his supporting hand which, in the interest of lining up squarely, is placed on the ground on a line just inside the foot (which is dropped back). The supporting arm will carry as much weight as the feet, and will be almost perpendicular with the shoulders and the ground. The opposite arm must be placed properly, or the lineman's shoulders will not be level. The correct position is for the wrist to rest across the thigh just above the knee, with the fingers hanging inside the knee.

The Back's Stance

The halfback's normal pattern enables him to break straight ahead with maximum speed, so that his stance is identical to the lineman's as previously described, though with one exception: The halfback's feet are split to the width of 6 inches. The fullback and quarterback, whose normal patterns of movement are lateral, will assume a stance with their feet parallel and spread the width of their shoulders. The fullback will place one hand on the ground but will have no weight on it. His weight is on the balls of his feet. The fullback is placed in the tripod position only because the stance makes it more difficult for the defense to key his initial movements, and he has less tendency to lean in anticipation of the count.

The quarterback's feet are slightly wider than the width of the shoulders and his toes are pointed out slightly. We like for the quarterback to crowd the center, in order that his hands may stay in position as the center charges out and the quarterback takes his initial step. Having the toes pointed out and outside of the center's feet helps the quarterback to execute his initial movement more effectively. The quarterback is as erect as he can be; he still places his hands properly, without disturbing the center's stance. One of the original concepts of the Split-T is that it is more difficult to block a tough defensive man than to take the ball, so the Split-T quarterback is required to adjust his stance to that of the center's.

The quarterback's top hand is placed under the center with the first finger in the middle of the crotch. The fingers are spread and slight pressure is exerted upward against the center to assure the proper hand position is retained during the initial step. The bottom hand is placed so that the wrist is tight against the wrist of the top hand, with the fingers spread and pointed toward the ground. Since the Split-T quarterback is asked to step out as he receives the ball, the high school coach should insist that the feet be wider than the center's, with toes pointed out. This helps the high school player to avoid the common tendency to step off the line to avoid the center's feet. Many high school quarterbacks take a circular step around the center's feet, which cuts down his speed and makes it difficult to reach the hand-off to the halfback.

Our chief concern is with the best methods of teaching the high school player to take his stance properly. Unless the coach is able to motivate a sense of pride in his players, his job of teaching them to assume the correct stance will be difficult. However, a boy of high school age can be made *stance-conscious* easily, for he quickly realizes that a good stance will make him look like a football player and set him apart from the scrub more quickly. One of the most discouraging problems confronting the coach is to teach the details of stance carefully to a player, only to find a few plays later he has slipped back into a sloppy position. The only answer that I have found is that most young men, through a desire to look like a football player, can be taught to correct these faults themselves. Build up that desire.

We call our first drill to teach stance the *Stance Check*. The players are lined up across the field and the coach goes down the line commanding each player to assume his stance. After the coach has made the necessary corrections, he sets the player off to a 5-yard sprint and moves down the line to the next player.

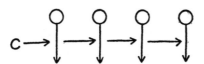

Fig. 1. The Stance Check.

After the players learn to assume a proper stance, the corrections can be made in a very short time, so the drill may be used at the beginning of each practice.

The second drill we use to teach stance is to line the players up in two lines facing each other, as illustrated in Figure 2. One line of players takes their offensive stances and the players opposite look them over critically, making suggestions how they might improve. The second line then takes the offense and is criticized by the first group.

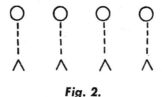

Fig. 2.

The third step in teaching stance is to install a full-length mirror in the dressing room so that it comes up the wall 4 feet and enables the players to check themselves. Once the player understands what his stance should be, the mirror will help him to conform to the proper stance more quickly than any drill.

In these drills, therefore, we have the coach checking the player's stance; the players checking each other's stance; and the players checking their own stance by using a mirror. A psychological coaching aid that works well on boys of high school age is to ask the seniors to help individuals who are inexperienced with their stances. Placing the responsibility on the seniors teaches them more than the youngsters they are trying to help. We know that in order to teach something you must know it, so the seniors will become conscious of every detail of a proper stance.

Lining Up on the Ball

Since it is imperative that the Split-T team take its proper position on the line of scrimmage, it is necessary for the coach to have some way of teaching the linemen how to accomplish this assignment effectively. It is not uncommon to see a team lined up with the guards a little behind the line, the tackles a little farther back, and the ends still farther behind their proper position. A team lined up in this manner is seriously handicapped, for considerable effort must be expended in regaining lost ground. The same effort, if the team had lined up correctly, would permit the offensive line to block the opponents on the defensive side of the line of scrimmage, assuring them of a successful play. The "sway-back" line will likely result, unless some definite method for lining up is given the team.

Fig. 3. Avoid the Sway-Back Line by properly lining up on the ball.

Our method of lining up on the ball has the linemen come out of the huddle to take a semi-erect position on the line of scrimmage. From this upright stance, with his hands on his knees, the lineman may look straight down to the ground. The guards sight an imaginary line that runs parallel to the line of scrimmage 1 foot behind the ball. The guards then place both hands on this line and from this position they kick their feet back to proper stance. This reverses the usual method of taking the stance, which is to position the feet first. Lining up on the ball is so important to the success of a team that we believe in positioning the hands to hold the proper alignment while feet are being positioned. When the guards have their feet properly placed, they lift one hand from the ground to complete their stance. The tackles and ends place their hands on a line with the hands of the guards and assume their stances in the same manner as the guards.

The imaginary line 1 foot behind the ball may be accurately established if the lineman will lean forward enough to look directly to ground. He measures 1 foot behind the ball and rolls his head out with his eyes following the line until he is looking straight down. With his hands on this line and in the stance described previously, he will be aligned properly. If this method is followed carefully, the undesirable sway-back line will be avoided.

High school players must be constantly reminded that they must line up properly. Our method helps the coach to spot the slovenly player, for unless he executes the tell-tale kickback of his feet every time he comes to the line of scrimmage, he is not carrying out his assignment properly. If the coach will position himself at the line of scrimmage during practice sessions like a headlinesman, he may check players during drills, signal running, and even at the start of wind sprints. Game movies are taken from the 50-yard line usually and afford the team an excellent opportunity to check its ability to line up on the ball.

As has been stated before, the most successful method for teaching high school players is to impress upon them the fact that the principles and techniques they are taught must be fully absorbed and learned by them if they are to win; the coach must motivate in them the feeling of pride that comes from looking like real football players when they execute the fundamentals properly.

Getting Off Together on the Snap

This is the most important fundamental in offensive football. For if a team is able to get off together on the count, it will make some yardage even though its blocking is poor. Since so much depends on the players' quick reaction to a starting signal, the Split-T coach should organize all of the practice session in such a way as to stress exploding into action on command. The starting count should be used in all drills, and if at all possible, the quarterback should call this starting signal. The quarterback starts all offensive action in games, so that the more often he gives the command in practice the better the reaction should be.

Careful planning will permit the squad to practice the execution of the starting count far more than is usually the case. The starting signal may be used in calisthenics or grass drills. In fact, in any situation where a group is learning or practicing drills, it should be brought to a starting position ready to explode into action with the quickest reaction possible. It should return after completing the exercise to go again. For example, if we were doing the simple exercise of bending at the waist to touch our fingers to our toes, we would have the squad stand upright at attention, start at top speed as the quarterback commands, complete the exercise as rapidly as possible, and return to original position ready for the next count. Any exercise that has a certain action that can be repeated after an interval of rest lends itself readily to our starting practice.

Wind sprints, if they are started by the quarterback calling the count and taking the ball from the center, work well in teaching the team to get off together on the snap of the ball. The ends, tackles, and guards should line up and go together, charging at top speed on the starting count in a game-like situation. The backs may do the same with good advantage even though they will not be concerned with lining up on the ball. However, it is imperative that the backs start on the count as well as the line, and all of the team should be impressed with the necessity of coming out low and hard.

No Rhythm or Cadence

It is my belief that high school boys respond better to a count called out of rhythm and without cadence. Cadence encourages the players to anticipate the count. They will often lean or roll into their charge when the count is called with regular intervals between commands. Leaning is not only illegal but it tips-off the defense that the ball is about to be snapped. If the defense can determine when the ball will be snapped, then one of the most important advantages of the Split-T offense has been lost. It is possible to coach well enough to call the count in cadence and not have the players leaning, but I believe we save time and get the desired results with the non-rhythm count. However, it seems best to be very irregular in calling the count in practice and more regular in a game. This is only part of the good rule for high school coaching: Do all of your *practicing during practice session. NEVER TRY ANYTHING IN A GAME THAT YOU HAVE NOT PRACTICED.*

Splitting the Line Effectively

Our objective in splitting the line is to put the defense at a disadvantage before the ball is snapped. If the defense spreads out with us as we split, it will have more territory to protect and will not be able to defend it as effectively as it would a small area. If the defense will not split with us, then it is going to give blocking angles. It follows that we can gain our advantage over the defense before the ball is snapped if we can split properly.

Just as has been true with the other Split-T fundamentals, the high school player must be thoroughly *sold* on the importance of splitting properly. The coach may start on the blackboard in the classroom to teach the linemen the common defenses and how to split for each defense. Here he may show the players that the quarterback is to move down the line less than a yard away from the defense on all basic plays and any penetration by the defense will likely cause a fumble.

No Penetration to the Inside of the Split

The coach must stress that every lineman has the prime responsibility of preventing a defender from penetrating to his inside. All linemen must know that the important rule for splitting is: If there is a defensive man playing to your inside between you and your teammate, you must close down your split to align your inside foot directly up the middle of the defender. This is the *safety-valve rule* of splitting and there will be no cases of penetration unless this rule is violated.

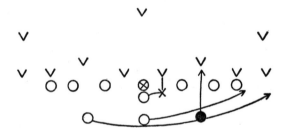

Fig. 4. Defensive penetration causes fumbles.

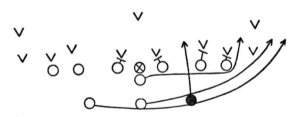

Fig. 4a. Close down on a defender playing to your inside.

The *safety-valve rule of splitting* is the first thing on the mind of the offensive lineman as he checks to his inside. If there is no defensive man in that position, he looks for the next opponent on the line of scrimmage. If the next opponent is outside of him, the offensive player should split out until the defensive man is playing head-on or he has taken a maximum split. I think that the high school coach should set a maximum, because of the tendency of the players to overdo the splitting. A maximum of 48 inches will work well in most cases. There are only two rules of splitting that the linemen need to know: *If there is a man inside, close down; if there is no man inside, take a maximum split.*

Figure 5 shows the application of these rules against

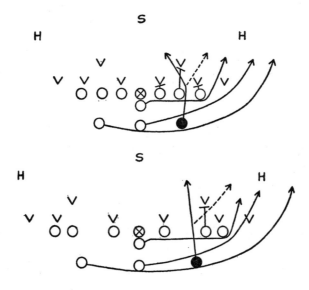

Fig. 5. Splitting spreads the defense and places them at a disadvantage.

the wide-tackle six defense. In this case, the defense moved with the splitting linemen and afforded the offense an opportunity to run between the defenders, who are forced to protect a lot of territory. In Figure 6 the defense men are assigned to play a certain distance from their teammates and will not split with the offense, but in this case the offense has the advantage of a blocking angle.

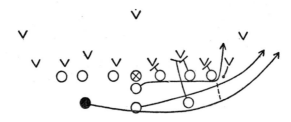

Fig. 6. Unless the defense splits with the offense, a blocking angle results.

To keep the problem of splitting on the lineman's mind, the quarterback should be instructed to call an imaginary defense. This will enable the offense to practice their splitting when the team is running signals, or when the line is running wind sprints.

If the entire squad is taught the common defenses, it will save time during the dummy scrimmage sessions. The reserves should be able to change defenses quickly every three or four plays to force the offense to change their splits. Careful planning will conserve practice time so that it will be possible for the offense to face a dozen defenses in short time. Since the rules for splitting are so simple, they can be applied to most defenses quickly.

Faking the Ball

As has been stated, faking well will keep the defense in doubt as to where the play will be run. Some of the situations where high school players are likely to shirk their faking should be stressed in order to build up the ability to fake. On the hand-off play when the halfback hits straight ahead into the line, the other three backs are likely to ease up too quickly and not carry their fake 5 yards downfield. If the outside defenders only see this trio running hard when they have the ball going wide, it will simplify their job of protecting the territory. If the three backs will fake hard on the hand-off play, the defense will be unable to key the wide play and will be slow in pursuing the inside play.

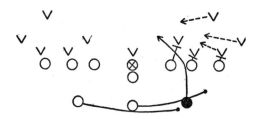

Fig. 7. With poor faking, the defense may pursue the play quickly.

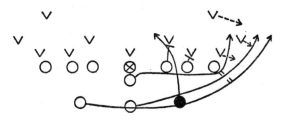

Fig. 7a. Good faking freezes the defense and slows their pursuit.

This situation may be improved by placing dummies 5 yards downfield and requiring the backs not carrying the ball to fake far enough to block these dummies.

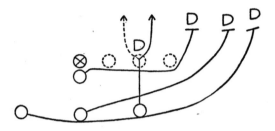

Fig. 8. Backs should carry their fake five yards downfield.

One of the hardest faking assignments is required of the Split-T lineman protecting the passer. If he comes up to the usual high pass-protection block, he immediately gives the pass away and makes it very difficult for the receivers to get open. The linemen must fire out on passes just as they do on running plays. The only solution seems to be to fire out, drop back very low, and fire out again until the pass is away. A helpful drill for Split-T pass protection is to have the linemen touch the ground after they have fired out and, while they are dropping back, to hit again. This action is helpful in teaching the linemen to stay low when performing the pass protection block. The coach should stress that the linemen should drag their fingers on the ground only as they are dropping back to repeat the action of striking out at their opponents.

The on-side halfback, who has the assignment of faking into the line on the wide play, can do his job better if he is taught to block into the line rather than fake into it. The halfback will in substance double-team with the tackle on his assignment by driving by on the outside of the offensive tackle on the wide play. I believe that the defense is rarely fooled by the maneuvers of the ball handler, so the main burden of faking falls on the players who do not have the ball.

3 | The Practice Schedule

ALL HIGH SCHOOL FOOTBALL COACHING, I believe, is a race against time. There are many demands on the players' and coaches' time. So if we are to teach all that is needed to play a game, we must plan carefully to use the time available as efficiently as possible.

In most cases, the high school coach can estimate with reasonable accuracy the time that he will have in the season ahead. The coach knows when practice will open; he knows when class work will start ending his two-a-day sessions; he knows when the players will be released from school; and he can figure how long he can keep them on the field. I believe that an hour and a half of practice, including warmup drills before and wind sprints at finish, is as long as we can expect high school players to be worked successfully.

In planning our practice schedules during the season, we find we have available in the average week (the

I prefer the two-man sled to the seven-man sled, because I can give individual attention to two men, whereas I can't see seven men in action at one time. I believe the most effective work can be done with a varsity of no more than 25 players. This allows the line coach to have the first two lines, the backfield coach to have two sets of backs. The remainder of the squad must be assigned to a "B" Squad. The last rule is:

3. No Lectures on the Field

When a coach stops the action to correct a mistake, he has 8 to 22 boys inactive while he points out the error to one player. This is a gross violation of the time rule, as all lecturing should be done in the class-room. If the players are not able to learn what they are to do in chalk talks, lecturing on the field will not help. This, of course, does not prohibit the coach from offering words of encouragement or criticism, if he can do it quickly and not delay the drill. On the field, players should be participants and not spectators.

Calisthenics

We start our drill by having the entire squad do calisthenics, led by the quarterbacks. Our players will not warm up sufficiently if left to their own initiative. We use the same exercises each day, for I think they can be performed faster as the players become familiar with the routine. The squad lines up in rows of eight and faces the two quarterbacks who take turns leading the drills.

actual game is played on Friday night) four sessions of one and a half hours in which to teach players all they need to know to play a game. It follows that the best method of presentation is to list all of the things we need to teach—offensive plays, pass defense, punting, kickoff, and so on through the list. Divide the list into four sessions, allowing more time for the important things. During the season, our first session would be on Monday, the second on Tuesday, and so on through the week, but in pre-season training we use the same schedule even in two-a-day periods. If our list included all that is necessary to play a game, then we would not change much during the season. In mid-season, we run signals instead of taking calisthenics, but we make no major changes. As we plan our schedule, we observe three rules:

1. No Standing in Long Lines.

A drill must have the players moving rapidly. There should be no long lines, for this not only wastes valuable time but encourages discipline problems. High school players tend to get their mind off what they are doing if the lines are long and often start horse-play when idle. The next rule is:

2. Work in Small Groups

No coach can watch 11 men in action at one time. For this reason not much coaching can be done in scrimmaging. In order to tell how the players are doing, it will be necessary for the squad to work in small groups.

Here is a brief description of the calisthenics that I recommend:

The Sag and Drag.   This exercise combines a stretch with the hands over the head with a body bend and push-ups. After the first stretch the players go to the push-up position, where they perform the body bends by sagging their hips to the ground. After five body bends they return to the upright position. Then they go down again to do five push-ups. Repeat the full set three times.

The Hurdle Spread.   The hurdle position is assumed on the ground. The players should attempt to touch their chins to the forward knee on the count and return to the body erect position. After ten counts the exercise is repeated with the other leg extended.

The Seat Roll.   The players assume the crabbing position on all fours with their knees up under them. On the count they roll over, touching their buttocks to the ground and on to the original position. On the next count the players roll in the opposite direction. Repeat 20 times.

Crabbing.   From the crabbing position on all fours, start on the count and run on a line parallel to the quarterbacks. The players continue to run in the crabbing position until they hear the count again, at which time they reverse to go in the opposite direction until the count. Better results can be obtained by requiring the players to turn their heads toward the quarterback on each reverse. Repeat 20 times.

Sit-ups and Leg Lifts.   The players do 10 sit-ups followed by 10 leg-lifts. During the leg-lifts the boys should not allow their feet to touch the ground, but should hold them about 6 inches off the ground between counts. They should not bring their legs up over them but should stop them when perpendicular to the ground. The quarterbacks determine how long the squad should hold their feet 6 inches off the ground by the length of the interval between counts.

Three Stretching Exercises.

1. Fold the arms across the chest and, bending at the waist on the count, try to touch elbows to the ankles while keeping the knees stiff. Repeat 10 times.
2. With the legs wide apart bend at the waist, throw arms between legs and try to touch the ground as far behind the feet as possible. Do not keep the knees stiff in this exercise. Repeat 10 times.
3. With the hands on ankles, the players try to touch their forehead to knees while keeping the knees stiff.

Three Rhythm Exercises.

1. The side-straddle-hop is a common exercise and no description is necessary.
2. The boxer's jump is started from a position of attention. The players move the right hand and foot forward at the same time. They return to the original position and repeat with the left hand and foot.

3. The cheer-leader is an exercise where the squad members kick their legs above their heads and slap their hands under their legs each time. The best results are obtained when the players are required to get their feet above their heads. All rhythm exercises should be repeated 20 times.

The Stance Step. From their offensive stance, the players step out into a blocking position with their chest tight against the right thigh. They then return to the offensive stance and repeat with their left leg up. Repeat the drill 10 times.

The Ape Hop. With the feet apart the width of the shoulders, bend sharply at the waist with only a quarter-bend at the knees, keeping the fingers touching the ground. Keeping the head up, hop one-quarter turn facing each direction, until you have hopped to the original position. On the next count go in the opposite direction.

Unit Drills

In the unit drills the players are divided into groups. The seven linemen make up the first group. The next group is the alternate line, and the remainder of the linemen are the third. A fourth group is composed of the first two backfields, and the last is the remaining backs.

The Wave Drill. In the wave drill each group lines up in a straight line facing the quarterback. Using hand signals, the quarterback points to the direction he wants the group to run. On signal the players break and run at top speed in one direction until the quarterback indicates a change. The signal should be changed rapidly from right to left, up and back, with the group moving at top speed. Seven or eight changes in direction are enough if speed is stressed. The drill should be repeated three times for each group.

Somersault and Form Tackle. Two groups are lined up 10 yards apart. One line takes a defensive stance on four points and on the count they quickly execute a somersault and form-tackle the players in the opposite line. The players should roll and regain their feet at top speed and the tackler should pick his man up and carry him 5 yards on his shoulder. Repeat the drill three times for each group.

Off on the Snap. This offensive drill stresses charging out hard and low on the count. The groups line up on the ball and go on the count with the center snapping the ball to the quarterback. It should be a 20-yard sprint with a coach at the finish line to pick the winners. A coach should check lining up on the ball and getting off together on the count. Each group takes five trials, with careful attention to proper execution of these fundamentals performed at top speed. The quarterback should be very irregular in calling the count during this drill, forcing the players to concentrate on the snap and preventing leaning in anticipation.

The calisthenics and unit drills are repeated each session. As the squad goes into the regular practice period, they are divided into "A" and "B" groups with the "A" linemen going to the line coach and the backs to the backfield coach. With the small groups established, the players are ready for the regular drills. This drill session is an hour in length each day, with the line and backs drilling separately. The ends go with the line two days for blocking practice, and with the backs two days for work on pass plays.

The last 30 minutes of each session is spent in team drills. Frequently we run a type of dummy scrimmage in which the first team is working against a defense made up of third-team players. The second offensive team faces the fourth team. This arrangement gives the two offensive teams an opportunity to run a great number of plays. Our type of dummy scrimmage has the defense coming in hard, playing off the blockers at full speed, but they are not permitted to tackle. I believe that we can do a great deal of this type of scrimmage with little danger of injury. The line play is almost game-like, and downfield blocking can be practiced every down since the ball-carrier will be down the field even when the defense is in a position to make the tackle behind the line. We insist that the defense tag the ball carrier and let him run 15 yards on every play.

As has been described, we like to start each group with the stance check. Regular checking emphasizes the importance of this fundamental and tends to make players more stance-conscious.

First Session

The line, including the ends, starts the first session with the sled drills. There are three sled drills and 30 minutes is assigned for a group of not more than 16 players. The players move at top speed, for we hope to increase their agility and balance by these drills.

The first sled drill has two players aligned in a stance with their knees on the ground. From this position they strike out on a count of "hit, hit, hit," trying to deliver a hard blow with their backs straight and the power coming from their hips. After the blow, the players should scramble back to their original position as quickly as possible, to be ready to strike again on a count that is given in a rapid-fire manner. After the third execution, the blockers do a seat roll and quickly regain their feet to shoulder-block a teammate 5 yards downfield.

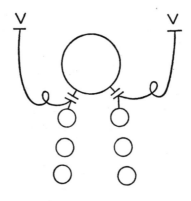

Fig. 9.

In the second sled drill the two players take an offensive stance. They hit out on the starting count just as they did in the first drill, but this time they do not move their feet, and go all the way to the ground on their chest. This lunging block develops maximum power and should bounce the sled a yard, if the two players get off together on the count. After each execution the blockers should scramble with utmost speed back to their offensive stance, to be ready to hit again on the rapid count. On the third command, the players strike the sled, regain their feet to do a somersault, and block a defensive player 5 yards down the field.

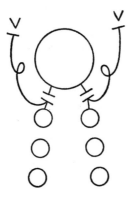

Fig. 10.

The third sled drill has the two players driving the sled from the goal line through the goal posts, circling one of the uprights and back to the goal line. Again speed is stressed as the blockers start from their offensive stance on the count and complete the trip as quickly as possible. The players should maintain good form as they drive the sled as fast as the short, digging steps they take will allow them. We make no attempt to develop leg power by loading the sled, since we are primarily interested in speed. The light sled is more difficult to control and the two players must learn to work together with balance if they are to handle it successfully.

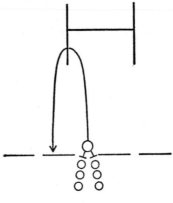

Fig. 11.

The Board Drill.   The last half of the line drills will be spent in blocking the dummies off the boards. The boards are two by twelves, 10 feet long. We use four such boards, with the dummies placed 1 yard from the end nearest the blockers. The blockers line up on the ends of the boards just as they do the ball. They charge out on the count and drive the dummies that are held by teammates off the boards in the shortest time possible. Sixteen players will keep the lines even and permit the right amount of rest as the players block five times with each shoulder. The boards emphasize the shoulder-width charging base for the blocker's feet and help to teach him to fire straight at his target.

The backfield drills the entire 60-minute period on the basic running plays. The group should run each play

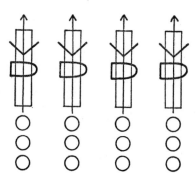

Fig. 12.

five times to each side of the line while using two complete backfields. The basic plays are: the Halfback Hand-off, the Fullback Counter, the Fullback Slant and the Option. Since every backfield operation starts with the center snap, we believe that the backfield drill should have a center to snap the ball to the quarterback. The coach should hold the dummy while the squad is working on the hand-off, slant, and counter, and he should be the defensive end while working on the option. These positions are the best for watching the ball handling and the faking. Since we are trying to hide the ball from the defense, the coach can judge the success better from a defensive position. Twice the amount of time should be devoted to practice of the option play since it is a very difficult one for a high school team to handle.

In the final portion of the session, the squad is divided into teams for dummy scrimmage. The first team will run all their plays against the third team, while the second team is pitted against the fourth. The offensive units

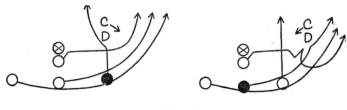

Fig. 13.

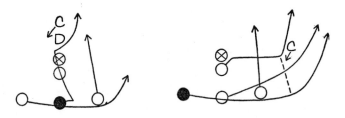

Fig. 13a.

are given the ball on the defense's 20-yard line and, in this no-tackling scrimmage, every play goes all the way to the goal line. The defensive teams are aligned in a head-up seven man line with a box secondary, and they are permitted to play the blockers hard, but must not tackle the ball carrier. Since every play goes the entire 20 yards, the drill is an excellent conditioner and permits concentration on downfield blocking.

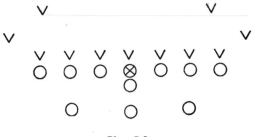

Fig. 14.

Second Session

The line starts the second session without the ends, who work with the backs during this period. Offensive drills are stressed as in the first session but no equipment such as sleds, dummies, or boards is used.

The five-on-five drill has the center, guards, and tackles facing five players in defensive positions. The offensive players are given the starting count in a huddle and the line coach calls the count after he has checked the players' ability to line up on the ball. It is good for a manager to take the snap from center, since we like the center to snap the ball every time he blocks. The objective of the offense is to drive the defense back a yard, whereas the defense merely tries to hit and hold. The players take five blocks with each shoulder.

Fig. 15.

The one-side blocking drill has the guard and tackle on one side of the line blocking two defenders who come in at full speed. This is an excellent drill for teaching the offensive men to hold their contact. They will not often be able to drive the defensive man off the line of scrimmage, but they will be able to turn him laterally if they hold their feet and keep contact.

With the same setup as the one-side blocking drill, the pass protection drill may be run. The Split-T line-

Fig. 16.

man has a difficult assignment keeping the defensive linemen off the passer, for unless he fires out and blocks low, he tips-off the defense that a pass is coming. The high-pass protection block that is used in other offenses does not faintly resemble any Split-T maneuver, so it would be a fine key for opponents. The maneuver we must use is to fire out on the count, drop back, staying low after contact and, as the defensive man comes in, hit again.

Fig. 17.

The center blocks during the next drill in a one-on-one setup. Here again the center will not be able to drive the defender off the line, but he should control him well enough for the ball-carrier to break by, if he keeps his feet and holds his contact.

Fig. 18.

The backfield with the ends will drill on their basic pass plays. Since all of our passes are play-passes—that is, they are passes that develop after the team goes through the basic operations of a running play—we try to fake well to conceal the intent to pass until the last second. Faking is stressed as the backs and ends drill on the Counter Pass, the Slant Pass, the Option Pass and the Swing Pass.

The team drills will find the squad in the same setup as the first session. The defense is required to change after six plays. There are two objectives that we hope to accomplish in this drill: First, the line will have to change their splits with each new defense and we hope they learn to split properly; and second, we expect the quarterback to recognize each defense and call plays that strike at the weakness of the defense. If the defensive team is taught all the common defenses, they can change quickly and a great number of plays can be run during the 30 minutes. It will also save time if the ball-carrier will stop when he is tagged by a defender who is in the position to make the tackle.

Third Session

The line starts its defensive drills with the forearm lift. The drill assigns two defensive men to use forearm lift on two offensive players to escape their blocks and move in to form-tackle two offensive players behind the line.

The players move into the shiver drill using the same setup as they used in the forearm lift. The shiver is a

Fig. 19.

straight-arm thrust with locked elbows that is com-
monly used by the middle guard. The defensive middle
guard has to cover the adjacent area on both sides of
the center. We feel that he should use the shiver since
it will prevent him from committing himself to either
side of the center. The drill is more effective if the offensive men are centers snapping the ball and the player
who is tackled would play the part of the quarterback.

Fig. 20.

Continuing with the same drill setup, the roll-out is
practiced. The roll-out is a maneuver designed to get
the defender back into the play after he is blocked out.
The line coach should caution the players not to use the
roll-out except in situation where the defensive man is
definitely out of the play, for there is a tendency on the
part of some players to fall off the line of scrimmage
when it would be better for him to hold his ground. I
think the greatest advantage of the roll-out drill is its

method of teaching agility and balance to a defensive lineman.

Fig. 21.

Bull-in-the-Ring must be closely supervised to prevent a player from being hit in the back and injured. Seven offensive blockers are stationed around a circle that has a radius of 2 yards. The defensive player takes the middle of the circle to ward off the blockers who come at him from all directions. The line coach should caution any offensive blocker to pull up and avoid the block if he is going to hit the defensive man in the back. When handled properly, Bull-in-the-Ring will teach a quick reaction on the part of the defensive player to protect himself.

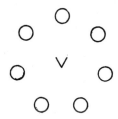

Fig. 22.

The reaction drills are last on our defensive schedule. The first of the four reaction drills has the defender playing in the gap between two offensive linemen. One of the offensive men blocks the defensive man, while the other pulls out of the line. The defender should play into the blocker to ward him off and follow the pulling lineman.

Fig. 23.

The next reaction drill places the defensive man in front of the center who is flanked by two guards. One of the guards blocks with the center to double-team the defender while the other guard pulls. The defensive lineman drives into the blocking guard and tries to move with the pulling lineman.

Fig. 24.

The third drill of this series is to teach the linemen to react to passes. The average lineman is satisfied if he does a creditable job of rushing the passer, so that as soon as the pass is thrown he becomes a spectator. This drill should impress the lineman that his assignment requires that he pursue the ball until the whistle blows.

The last of the reaction drills is a team drill for all the line and linebackers. The defensive line should key the

Fig. 25.

movement of the offensive linemen and make the proper adjustments. Determining the reaction of the linemen, rather than the backfield, is the most accurate method of predicting what the offense plans to do.

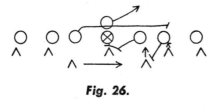

Fig. 26.

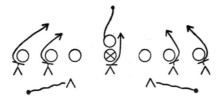

Fig. 26a.

The backs and ends will devote their drill period during this session to pass defense. Our first pass defense drill is the interception drill. The defensive back takes his station facing the quarterback about 6 yards deep. He drops back quickly when the pass is indicated by the quarterback dropping to position. The defensive back should reach the area he is to protect by the time the quarterback has reached his throwing position. When the passer throws the ball, the defensive player should break quickly and race at top speed for the ball. If he can make the interception, he should catch the ball as high as possible and run for the nearest sideline. If the defensive team is using the zone pass defense, this drill is good because it teaches the players to watch the ball with no receivers coming down the field.

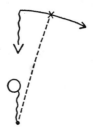

Fig. 27.

The individual pass defense drill is set up like the interception drill, with the exception that we send two receivers about 6 yards deep. The receivers start on the count and run down the field, keeping approximately 30 yards apart while the defender breaks back, staying directly between them. When the ball is thrown, the defensive man breaks to the ball at top speed. I believe that better results will be obtained if the receivers are so wide that they will not collide with the defender as he goes for the ball. The objective is to see how far the defensive man can run while the ball is in the air. The average boy will not go full speed after a collision. To do well, the secondary man must stay in the middle, keep his eyes on the passer, react quickly to the throw, and run at top speed for the ball.

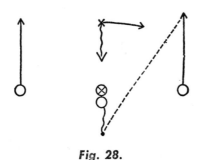

Fig. 28.

The "Play-the-Quarterback" drill is to teach the secondary to key the various movements of the quarterback. Both of the normal alignments are used—the box defense and the three-deep. As the quarterback moves out from the center to indicate the direction of the play, the secondary makes the proper adjustments.

During the last portion of the drill period, the secondary defends against a skeleton offensive unit made up of the two ends and complete backfield. The defense is deployed in both alignments, the box and three-deep, during the drill.

The team drills for the third session are spent in kicking. We divide the time among three phases: punting, kick-off, and extra-points. We try to stress our protection and coverage but do not try to coach the kickers during

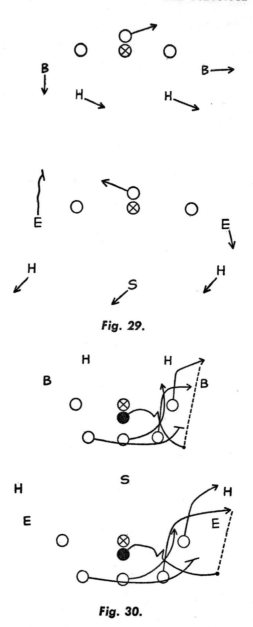

Fig. 29.

Fig. 30.

this 30-minute period. The kickers must work on their specialties in off season, for we can't teach him more than his team assignment in the rush of practice.

Fourth Session

The line with the ends repeats the sled drills and the board drills that they ran in the first session, but cut the time to 20 minutes for each drill. This gives the linemen time to work on their blocking for such special plays as traps and reverses.

The backs work on the special plays during the first part of their drill and take the last half of this session to work again on the difficult option play. It is necessary to spend extra time on this play if a high school team is going to be able to handle it successfully. Unless the option play can be perfected, there is little point in using the remainder of the Split-T attack, for the opponents will be aligned so tightly that it will be impossible to move the ball well on the hand-off, slant, and counter.

The team drills for the fourth session will be checking our defense against our opponent's offense. A reserve team is lined up in the offensive formation to make certain the defense is ready for statues, screens, and delayed passes to blockers. We like to be certain of our assignments against flankers, spreads, and unusual formations, so we have our reserves run these formations for our defense.

This drill system of practice does not appeal to all coaches, but we have used it and are well satisfied. One coach told me that he couldn't use the schedule because he practiced kicking 30 minutes every day. I recognize that we have a weakness, but since our theory is that games are won by the team that maintains possession of the ball the majority of the time, I think we should concentrate on maintaining possession. When you kick, you give up the ball. In the final analysis, however, I do not devote more time to kicking simply because I wouldn't be able to decide what to eliminate from the hour and a half of drills in order to devote more time to kicking. This is the reason for leaving a number of things out of the schedule.

Teaching Split-T
Fundamentals to the Line

THE PROBLEM FACING THE SPLIT-T LINE-
man in high school is in learning *how* to block rather
than knowing *whom* he should block. The coach should
concern himself with teaching the fundamentals of the
Split-T line play, inasmuch as he does not have to devote time to blocking assignments, since the player
blocks the man in front of him 90 per cent of the time.

Players should recognize that the fundamentals that
make us go are:

1. Assuming the correct stance.
2. Splitting properly.
3. Lining up on the ball.
4. Getting off together on the count.
5. Firing right at the opponent, making low, solid
   contact and staying on our feet to maintain contact.

Since the blocking assignments are so simple that they
may be boiled down to mean *"block the man in front of
you,"* some linemen may ignore them altogether. A fa-

mous university line coach tells the story of a lineman who had one answer everytime he was asked, "What do you do on this play?" "I fire right at him," was the player's standard reply. The coach confused the lineman on one occasion by asking, "You fire at whom?" Actually a Split-T lineman would be correct most of the time with the statement, "I fire right at the man in front of me."

The straight-shoulder block is the fundamental block of the offense. The quick, straight-ahead attack of the Split-T does not lend itself readily to body blocking, leg blocking or any type of tie-up blocking. Our lineman aims the middle of his forehead at the belt buckle of his opponent or, if the defensive player is down in a four-point stance, he aims at the opponent's chin. Let us review the essentials of a good shoulder block.

The first move of the offensive lineman is designed to *hit the defender on the defensive side of the line* of scrimmage. We must engage the defense on their side of the ball if our quarterback is to move down the line. If our linemen get the idea of really taking off, we have most of the battle won. If we fail and our quarterback is driven off the line, we have lost most of our ability to move the ball.

The second detail is to fire right at the opponent and make solid contact. Our lineman must never step for position. To do so will lead the opponent to step out in the same direction and we will close the hole that we are trying to open. Note in Figure 31 that when the right guard steps for position, the defender keys this action and moves toward the path of the ball-carrier.

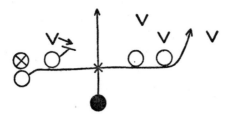

Fig. 31.

We should never try to move the opponent in any direction, but should take him the *easy way*. The *easy way* is the direction the opponent wants to go. The Split-T attack is fluid enough so that the ball-carrier can cut behind the block when the defender is driven on past the hole by the offensive lineman who has fired right at him. (See figure 32.)

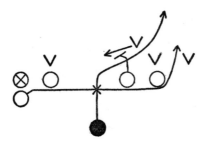

Fig. 32.

We will not block with our forearm or elbow if we aim the center of our forehead at the defender's belt buckle, but will make solid contact by aiming right through the middle of the opponent. This is the action that draws the praise of college line coaches who are always seeking the boy who is willing to *stick his head in*.

The next essential is to maintain contact with the opponent. After the initial block has been made, every effort should be expended to hold the contact and keep the defender engaged until we can move the ball by him. We fail most often in this assignment by going to the ground, so we should hold our feet with short, digging steps and keep our head and shoulders in contact on a line aimed through the center of the opponent's body.

The last step is to raise the shoulders slightly and drop the tail as the defender is forced to retreat. Trying to maintain the low position of the initial contact will result in falling to the ground. Raising gradually after the contact puts the offensive lineman in a favorable position to move quickly downfield to help clear the way if the ball-carrier gets past the line of scrimmage.

The Hand-off

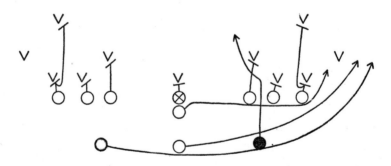

Fig. 33. Hand-off VS 5-4-2.

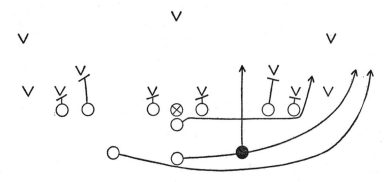

Fig. 33a. Hand-off VS Wide Tackle 6.

The hand-off is the basic play of the Split-T offense. The defense must be made to respect this play and protect the inside area where it strikes. The quick striking power of the hand-off forces the defense to dig in solidly or be driven back by the aggressive linemen. Since the initial steps of every basic Split-T play are identical, the defenders must defend against the hand-off and are in poor position to pursue on wide plays.

The offensive strategy of the Split-T in high school is not to outsmart or trick the defense but to hit them so hard, so suddenly, and so aggressively that they will be unable to withstand the force of our attack. The hand-off is our principal weapon for this purpose. Unless the opponents align six defensive men inside our offensive ends, the hand-off is the spearhead of our attack. If the defense is so heavily fortified to the inside, they must be vulnerable elsewhere, since they have only five men to defend the flanks and to cover our passes.

If the linemen know the split-rule, the blocking assignments are very simple. Note in Figure 33 how the splitting of the offensive linemen has simplified their assignments.

To repeat—the ingredients of a successful hand-off play are: assuming the correct stance, splitting properly, lining up on the ball, getting off together on the count and firing right at the opponent.

The Counter

The Fullback Counter Play is designed to take advantage of the defense if they should move laterally to rein-

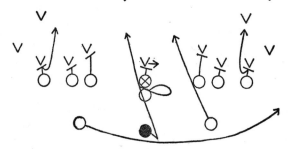

Fig. 34. Counter VS 5-4-2.

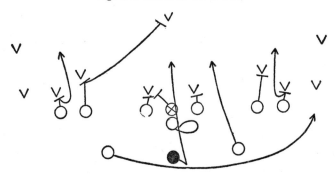

Fig. 34a. Counter VS Wide Tackle 6.

force the point of attack for the hand-off. The blocking on this play is exactly the same as for the hand-off, so we believe the defense will be confused if they are keying the linemen.

The 5-4-2 defense illustrated in Figure 34 is the defense that we see most often. Our splitting has isolated the defensive middle guard; as a point of strategy the counter play is indicated when this defender pursues the halfback quickly on the hand-off. The offensive center, by blocking directly at the middle guard, merely helps him along as he goes for the backfield fake of the counter play and the ball can be moved well on the other side.

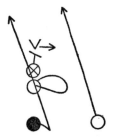

Fig. 35.

When the offense is faced with the wide-tackle six, the defender in front of the off-side guard is being pulled toward the ball by the backfield fake so he is double-teamed by the guard and center. The fake of the halfback pulls the defender in front of the on-side guard away from the ball-carrier. In fact, if the halfback will drive by on the outside of the offensive guard, he will in substance double-team this defender with the guard.

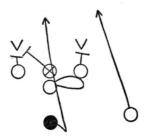

Fig. 36.

The Fullback Slant

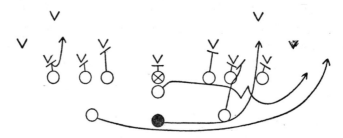

Fig. 37. Slant VS 5-4-2.

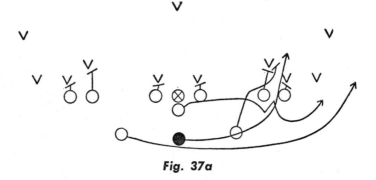

Fig. 37a

On the Fullback Slant the linemen are driving directly
at the defender in front of them, exactly as in their block-

ing on the hand-off and the counter. The operation of
the linemen does not differ on any of the basic plays,
so it is very difficult for the defense to key its blocking
to determine the point of attack.

The backfield will be faking a wide play on the slant,
so that the end will have the help of this fake to pull
his man away from the path of the ball-carrier. If, however, the defensive man on the end does not take the
fake of the backfield and drives to inside, it will not
hamper the play. The end should hold his contact and
take the defender on to the inside, the way he wants to
go. The fullback can make the adjustment and cut to
the open side after he gets the ball.

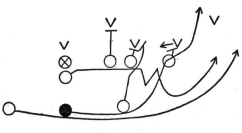

Fig. 38.

The tackle will find his man playing slightly to his
outside on both of these defenses. Since the path of the
ball-carrier is to his outside also, it would appear that
he would have a very difficult task keeping this defensive player from stopping the play. However, if the opponent is a good player, his reaction to the straight-ahead
block of the offensive tackle will be to drive back into
the blocker. Most well-coached defensive teams will

meet strength with strength, so we may expect this defender to meet the tackle's aggressive block with an equal force. This action will give the halfback, who is driving into the line just to the tackle's outside, an opportunity to hit the defender while he is engaged in resisting the offensive lineman's block. In reality, the offense has a double-team block by the tackle and halfback on this defensive man.

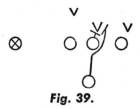

Fig. 39.

The blocking of the linemen will be easier and more effective if the offensive team can establish a threat of running wide. The Slant is basically a cut-back off the same operation that is used by the offense to run wide around the ends, so the defense must fear the end run before they will take the fake and leave the off-tackle territory vulnerable to the Slant Play.

The Option Play

We have established the fact that in the majority of assignments the Split-T lineman blocks the man in front of him. But we now note an exception: We have one player on the option play who leaves the man in front to block to his inside. This player is the on-side end who double-teams with the tackle. The quarterback makes the trip out to the defensive end, staying right on the line of scrimmage. Any penetration by the defensive linemen would reach the quarterback and may cause a fumble. This is one reason we dropped the man-for-man blocking on the option play.

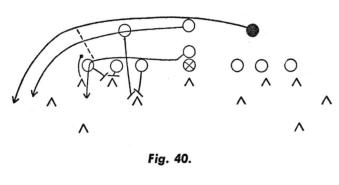

Fig. 40.

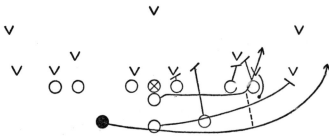

Fig. 40a.

Another reason for leaving the standard assignment of blocking to the man in front is that when faced with the 5-4 defense diagrammed in Figure 41, and several other common defensive alignments, the man-for-man blocking leaves no defender on the line of scrimmage for the quarterback to play. If, as the quarterback moves down the line, he can see no defender, he is seriously handicapped in his operation. The offensive end will be unable to hold his man-for-man block until the quarterback can turn the corner, and the defensive man usually hits the quarterback unexpectedly.

In order to give the quarterback a fair chance with the defender, the offense should move out of his line of vision and leave the defender isolated in order that the quarterback may watch him relentlessly from his first step.

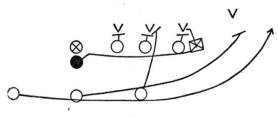

Fig. 41.

The reason why high school teams fail to execute the option play successfully more often is not so much due to poor operation by the quarterback as it is that they fail to set up their blocking properly. Recently there has been a tendency to seek a simplified version of the option play for what some coaches call a run-of-the-mill quarterback. We feel that the Split-T quarterback does not have to be better than the quarterback in any other formation if we, as coaches, make our plans definite enough to give him a chance with the defense.

There are a few principles that we must set up in the

line to operate the option successfully: We must split our line so that the offensive end is about the same distance from the center on every defense. The quarterback should reach the option-defender at the same distance all of the time, against all defenses. We must devise a type of double-team on all inside defenders to assure that there will be no penetration to prevent the quarterback from moving down the line. We must leave a man for the quarterback to play. This means that the offensive end blocks in on the option play at all times, leaving any defender who plays in front or outside of him for the quarterback.

By observing these principals of line blocking, the distance from the center to the point where the quarterback will encounter the defensive end will not vary with each defense, and the quarterback can perfect his operation much more easily.

Developing the Backfield
For Basic Split-T Plays

T HE BACKFIELD HAS CERTAIN IMPORTANT
fundamentals that will supersede other assignments.
Several of these are the same fundamentals that are emphasized for the linemen. The rules that the linemen
share with the backs are:

1. Each back must have a *good stance* in order to
   start quickly. Defensive linemen cannot be blocked
   for long periods of time. Therefore the back must
   be able to break quickly on the count to rush the
   ball by the defender while he is still engaged with
   the blocker.

2. The back must *line up properly* in relation to the
   positions taken by the linemen. If the back is to
   receive the ball from the quarterback at the same
   spot each time, he must line up properly.

3. The backfield must *get off together* with the remainder of the team on the starting count. The
   offense knows when the ball will be snapped. The

defensive team does not. To exploit this advantage fully the backs must break quickly on the starting count.

There are two more fundamentals that are required of the backfield that have not already been assigned to the line. These rules that apply only to the backfield are:

1. Each back should carry his *fake 5 yards downfield*, unless he is tackled. When faking well, the back will almost certainly be hit, but he should never duck, never slow up, and he should always hit the proper hole. Since the quarterback is moving the ball along the line, our faking starts at the line of scrimmage and extends 5 yards downfield.

2. Every back must know exactly where the *exchange point*—the spot where he receives the ball from the quarterback—is located. Since the back must be watching the blocking ahead and must not look at the ball the moment the quarterback gives it to him, he must run directly to the exchange point.

The Halfback

The halfback should take a stance that will enable him to move forward with the greatest possible speed. He should constantly check his stance. Here are the details of a proper stance for the halfbacks: The feet are 6 inches apart and the right toe is dropped back to the heel of the left foot; the right hand is on the ground in front of the right foot with considerable weight on it; the left forearm is across the thigh with the fingers hanging inside the knee; the halfback's head is up; his back is straight and like a sprinter in track the halfback's tail is high so that he does not have to raise it to start.

The lateral spacing of the halfback's position does not vary in the high school Split-T. This rule will differ from the method taught by most colleges, which change the lateral spacing of the halfbacks with each defense. Obviously, each time the halfback changes his lateral position, he must also change his depth from the line of scrimmage. The farther the halfback splits away from the fullback, the deeper he must be to intersect the path of the quarterback at the same time. (See Figure 42.)

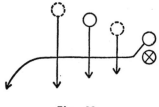

Fig. 42.

It is my opinion that it would take so much time to teach these two adjustments to high school players that it would not be time well spent. By establishing a definite lateral position for the halfback, he can learn his depth from the line of scrimmage much easier. With the spot where he takes his stance remaining constant, the halfback can automatically learn to line up well in a game.

Since the halfback lines up directly behind the *exchange point*, the location of this exchange point must be determined accurately. The best method for finding the exact spot is have the guard split away from the center one foot, and the tackle split 2 feet. With this alignment, the exchange point will be directly beneath the outside hip of the tackle. Until the halfback learns this position well enough to find it without the linemen, it is good to have the guard and tackle take this preliminary split as they come out of the huddle each time, so that the inexperienced halfback may line up correctly. In all drills where the backfield may be working independently of the line, the exchange point must be established accurately in order that the halfback will become so familiar with his position that he will automatically line up correctly.

The Fullback

The fullback will line up 4 to 4½ yards from the line of scrimmage directly behind the quarterback. The stance of the fullback has the feet on the same line with a wide, comfortable base about the width of the shoulders. The right hand is on the ground but there is no weight on it. The left forearm is across the knee and the weight is on the balls of his feet. The fullback's head is up. When he starts, the fullback simply throws his head and shoulders in the direction he wants to go, and steps out with the foot on the side to which he is going. He should never use a cross-over step, but should split his stance for his first step. His first move must be directed at a point 3 yards in front of the defensive end. The fullback must never lean in the direction of the play before the count, and he must be certain that he is giving the defense no indication as to the direction of the play prior to the snap.

The Quarterback

As the quarterback takes his stance, he should crowd the center and retain as high and comfortable a position as possible. Do not bend the knees more than is necessary to place the hands without disturbing the center's stance. The feet should be in line, split wider than those of the center and the toes should be pointed out slightly. The position should be relaxed and should be balanced with the weight equally distributed on both feet. Since the defense keys the quarterback more often than any other offensive player, he should check himself regularly for *tip-offs* to the direction he is going to move on the snap.

The quarterback's hands should be placed in such a position that the index finger of the right hand is down the middle of the center's crotch. The heels of the hands should be together and the fingers should be spread and relaxed. The tips of the fingers of the left hand should point directly to the ground. Since the quarterback is crowding the center, he can retain this hand position for 18 inches merely by extending his arms.

The first move of the quarterback on each play is identical. As the snap is called, he should step up and out with the foot on the side to which he is going. While doing this, his hands should follow the center forward. The quarterback's hands should maintain their original position on the center's crotch until the ball hits.

Before the start of any drill session the quarterback should take several snaps from the center and move out to both sides. To make this practice realistic, the center should always charge out to block with each snap. Since the Split-T lineman fires out on every play, the ball exchange between the center and quarterback will not be authentic unless the center is moving out on the snap.

With·the center charging out, the quarterback must remember as he practices that he has a double movement to make when he calls the snap. He is stepping up and out with the foot on the side where the play is going. He is extending his arms to keep his hands in position in the center's crotch while the center moves away from him.

Most fumbles occur on the exchange because the quarterback's hands do not follow out until he actually receives the ball. This operation must be practiced faithfully until the quarterback can take the ball from the center while making his double movement without a bobble.

The quarterback should be taught to check himself on several important fundamentals that mean the success or failure of his operation on each play. He should look for and correct these most common errors in his operation that cause fumbles in the ball exchange with the center. Since the ball is snapped to start each play, a team that fumbles the center exchange is "dead" offensively before it starts. Here are the points on which the quarterback must check himself:

1. Unless the quarterback is crowding the center, the center will charge away from the quarterback's hands and he will not be able to reach far enough to maintain proper hand position under the center's crotch.

2. If the quarterback pulls his hands back as he takes the lateral step, he will again lose hand position.

3. The center is snapping the ball and charging out at the same time, so the quarterback must follow him to maintain good hand position. He must step as he calls the snap.

4. The step must be *up and out*. If the quarterback steps back on the first step, he will probably give more ground on the second step, which will cause him to leave the line of scrimmage and ruin the play.

5. The quarterback must stay on the line of scrimmage. Unless he moves along the line of scrimmage and hands-off the ball right on the line or better a little ahead of the line, our attack will be hitting too slowly and will not be successful.

The Drill for the Hand-off Play

The equipment that I suggest in this drill is a board and standard upright dummies. The board is a one by six, and is 3 feet 6 inches in length. The purpose of the board is to teach the backs to run with their feet apart.

With the board placed so that the ball-carrier must run over it, he must have his step more than 6 inches apart

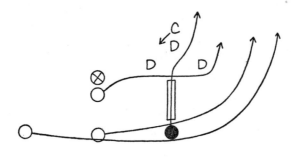

Fig. 43.

or step on the board. This type of running will enable the back to cut more sharply. The board is very helpful to the inexperienced player in locating his exact lateral spacing. It also teaches the ball-carriers that they must run directly for the exchange point with no cutting or veering from their course until the ball is in their possession. The dummies are the large, heavy bags that will stand upright without being held by a player.

The drill for the hand-off play is set up with the board placed so that the forward end will be over the exchange point. The method of locating the exchange point for the hand-off play has already been described, but the transfer point must be made accurately or the timing of the drill will be off. The exact spot of the transfer of the ball from the quarterback to the halfback is the outside hip of the tackle. The latter has taken a 2-foot split away from the guard, who has a 1-foot split. The halfback will take his stance directly behind the rear end of the board.

The backfield coach should take his position behind the middle dummy. During the drill the coach steps out from behind the dummy after the ball has been snapped, forcing the halfback, who is watching his movement, to cut in the opposite direction.

I believe this is the best position for the coach to watch the action in the drill. He may control the situation from this point by stepping out quickly for the inexperienced player. If the ball-carrier has developed his ability to cut, the coach may wait until the halfback has reached the exchange point before making his move. I think it is a mistake for the coach to move the dummy or to lean it from the top to indicate the direction he wants the ball-carrier to take. We are trying to teach the halfback to watch the movement of the defensive player, whose role the coach is playing. We do not want the ball-carrier to cut away from the offensive blocker represented by the dummy. Although the coach may be run over occasionally by an inexperienced player, he should never assign his position behind the middle dummy to a player. A player will lose control of the situation and will not be able to point out the mistakes as the coach should be able to do from this vantage point.

Let us consider the *operation of the quarterback* on the hand-off drill. Assuming that the quarterback takes the correct stance, he should step up and out as he calls the snap. After he receives the ball, the quarterback should concentrate on the outside hip of the halfback. It will be necessary for the quarterback to reach far out in order to place the ball securely in the ball-carrier's pocket. If the quarterback's arm is not fully extended, the play is too slow. When the halfback is hitting quickly, the quarterback's arm will be completely extended.

When the quarterback sees that he is not able to reach the far hip of the halfback, he should not try to give the ball off but should keep it himself. The play will be far more successful when the quarterback keeps the ball and follows the halfback into the line than it will be if he tries to hand it off when he can't reach the halfback's outside hip. Often fumbles occur as a result of the ball striking the inside hip of the halfback when the quarterback tries to hand-off the ball when he is unable to reach the pocket.

The quarterback should operate straight down the line and should not look back at the halfback after he has transferred the ball to him. He will add to his faking and make the play more successful if he will look at the opposite halfback coming around as he reaches the option area. At this point, the quarterback should fake a lateral to the halfback and cut squarely to continue his fake well up the field.

In the drill the *halfback* who is going to carry the ball should take his stance directly behind the board and the exchange point. As the ball is snapped, the halfback breaks straight-ahead with all possible speed. With his hands in the proper position, he will receive the ball at the same spot each down. By taking short steps and having his feet 6 inches apart, the halfback should be able to make the proper cut. His head should be up and his eyes on the movement ahead.

The *fullback* should start on the snap for the point 3 yards in front of the defensive end. He should run hard on this course and continue to carry his fake 5 yards downfield.

The *opposite halfback* should start on his normal course of coming around just as he does on the option play. He should run hard and be in position to receive the lateral in order to make the best fake possible. The halfback must also carry his fake well down the field.

Since the faking is so important to the success of the hand-off play in order to keep the outside defenders from closing in on the ball-carrier, placing three dummies 5 yards downfield for the three faking backs to block will help. The quarterback, fullback, and opposite halfback must be impressed with the necessity of running their course hard to a position 5 yards beyond the line of scrimmage, so the addition of the three dummies will help considerably.

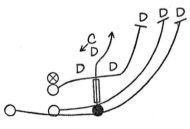

Fig. 44.

The Drill for the Counter Play

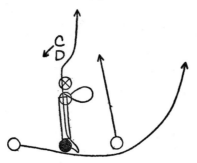

Fig. 45.

The board is used in the counter play drill, but I believe it is best to use only one dummy. This is the middle dummy, which is used by the coach to stand behind to observe the action and signal the direction of the ball-carrier's cut. In this drill the other two dummies would crowd the center. If the center blocks during this drill, he cuts off the coach's view of the ball handling. The best results are obtained when the center charges out fast to one side. The objective of the drill is to teach faking, ball handling, and cutting to the backfield. The coach must have an unobstructed view of the action in order to give his constructive criticism.

The drill is set up with the board pointed from a point between the feet of the fullback to the left foot of the center. If the hand-off is faked on the right, the exchange point for the counter play will be the left foot of the offensive center. When the left halfback is faking the hand-off, the exchange point for the counter play will be the right foot of the center.

I think the timing of the play is aided by the fullback moving a half yard closer to the line of scrimmage to take his stance. Since the fullback should make a head and shoulder fake toward the side line before he starts forward, he will delay his start forward. It is necessary for the fullback to hit quickly so we line him up 18 inches closer. This position will also put the fullback ahead of the path of the halfback, who must break around behind him faking the option play.

The *quarterback* steps up and out on the snap in his normal manner as he starts the counter. His second step is very short. A deliberate effort should be made to stop his second step even with his other foot. This is a difficult assignment when the quarterback is moving as rapidly as is necessary on this play. We suggest that the quarterback try to dig the cleats of his left heel into the turf and he may be able to stop the foot short enough.

As his second step is planted, the quarterback should bend sharply at the waist and thrust his left hand as far out as he can, trying to touch the faking halfback. The ball is held with the right hand in the quarterback's stomach.

The third step is a pivot of 270 degrees to place the ball on the far hip of the fullback. After the hand-off the quarterback completes his maneuver by dropping back to fake a pass.

The ball must stay on the line of scrimmage during the entire operation of the quarterback. He must not hand the ball back to the fullback but must actually make the hand-off forward to the fullback who has al-

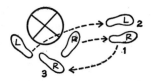

Fig. 46.

ready passed him. If the ball is given to the fullback behind the line of scrimmage, the defense will have time to adjust to the play.

Another detail that must be observed by the quarterback is that he must keep the ball at hand-off level during his entire operation. He should not move the ball up and down, but slide it into the fullback's pocket after carrying it at the proper height in his stomach. Often a quarterback will try to bring the ball up from underneath to place it on the far hip. The fullback may strike the ball with his knees if the hand-off is too low.

The *fullback* makes his first move from his close position as if he were going to run his normal course. He should make his fake by throwing his head and shoulders quickly toward the sideline. Completing his fake quickly, the fullback should head directly for the exchange point. He should take the ball with his head up and his eyes on the blocking ahead. The fullback should have the same hand position to receive the ball and should carry it exactly as has been described for the halfbacks.

The *halfback* drives forward exactly as he does on the hand-off. He must hit closer to the center in order for the quarterback to touch him as he fakes giving the ball to him. To make the fake more effective, the halfback must be certain that he is hitting the right hole. If the opponents are in a defense with a middle guard in front of the offensive center, the halfback's job is to help pull this defensive guard away from the path of the fullback. When faced with an even defense, the halfback must fake the defender in front of the offensive guard away from the play. (See Figure 46.)

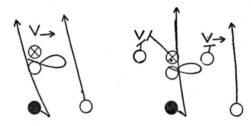

Fig. 47. Odd defense.   **Even defense.**

The *halfback* on the side away from the play must fake around in his normal manner. Although the fullback is closer to the line of scrimmage on the counter play than he normally would be, the halfback must be careful not to bump into the fullback while he is faking.

The Drill for the Slant Play

The exchange point of the slant play is the inside foot of the offensive end. When this point is established, the coach moves his three-dummy setup over in front of the spot. The coach uses the dummies exactly the same as he does in the hand-off drill.

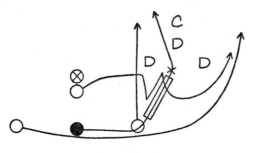

Fig. 48.

The first two steps of the *quarterback* are made with fake of the hand-off play. The first step is the normal up-and-out step as the quarterback receives the ball; the second step is long. On the second step, as the foot strikes the ground, he should drop his head and shoulders as if to hand the ball to the halfback.

The third step is off the line at a 45-degree angle. On the fourth step, the quarterback brings his feet together and faces away from the line of scrimmage at 45 degrees.

As the fourth step is taken, the lateral to the far halfback is faked by swinging the ball back to arm's length to show it to the defensive end behind the full-back. The quarterback will make his operation more effective if he will train himself to carry the ball on a plane horizontal to the ground at hand-off height throughout the maneuver.

The fifth step is to reach the spot where the quarterback transfers the ball to the fullback. It is a very long step directly toward the exchange point. To extend himself beyond his reach the quarterback should bend sharply at the waist to bring his chest down on his knee. The long step and lunge out on the forward knee is essential in order to reach the fullback's far hip. If the ball is shown to the defensive end behind the fullback, the fullback will have already passed the quarterback and the long reach is necessary to get the ball in front of the fullback.

While the quarterback is making his fifth step, the ball should be brought from the extreme point of the lateral fake back into his stomach and thrust out again to the fullback. A mistake that is often made by the quarterback is to swing the ball around to the fullback. This action results in the ball striking the ball-carrier in the back. With the quarterback actually holding the ball until the fullback has passed as the fake of the play requires, he must bring the ball back into his stomach in order to move it around the fullback and into the ball-carrier's pocket.

The quarterback's operation on the play is completed by faking on out around the end.

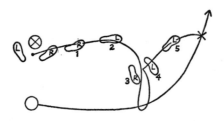

Fig. 49. Steps of the Quarterback on the Slant Play.

The *fullback* should start in his usual manner on a course that runs 3 yards in front of the defensive end.

Remembering that the exchange point is the inside foot of the offensive end, the fullback should watch that spot out of the corner of his eye while trying to make the defense believe he is going wide.

The fullback cuts on his third step and runs directly over the exchange point. As he arrives at the spot where he is to receive the ball, he must make certain that he has the proper hand position so the quarterback can give him the ball without a slip-up. With his head up and his eyes on the movement ahead, the fullback should make the proper cut to the open side.

The *halfback* on the side where the play is directed has a double movement to make. He must fake the hand-off play and he must aid in the blocking. The best method of meeting this double assignment is to drive by just outside the offensive tackle exactly as if he were carrying the ball.

If there is a defensive man playing to the outside of the tackle, the halfback will help the offensive blocker with his task materially. However, it is imperative for the lineman to accept the full responsibility for blocking the defensive player and not expect the halfback to share equally in a double-team block. To do so results in the halfback hitting too slowly and clogging up the hole. A successful operation can be expected if the halfback runs like a ball-carrier with all the power he can muster just outside the offensive tackle. If no defensive man is playing in this area, the halfback should break through the line to block a secondary opponent downfield.

The *halfback* from the opposite side has one major responsibility. He must put himself in the best position to fake taking the lateral from the quarterback. This means that he must run hard to the lateral area and continue his fake until it has carried him 5 yards downfield.

The Drill for the Option Play

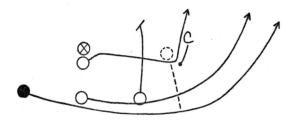

Fig. 50.

The backfield coach sets up the option play drill without any equipment such as dummies or boards. The coach may find his place by lining up slightly to the outside of the spot where the offensive end would take his position.

I think that it is more important for the coach to play the part of the defensive end on the option play drill than it is for him to stand behind the dummy on the other drills. An inexperienced quarterback can be discouraged easily if the person playing the defensive end tried hard at first to beat him. The coach should begin making definite moves and not try to slap the lateral down until the quarterback can learn his operation. After the quarterback has learned the maneuver, the coach may play him a little harder but he should never turn this assignment over to a player. Whenever a player is given the assignment of playing defensive end against the option play, he should go full speed and the fullback should be allowed to block him if he is on the spot.

The *quarterback's* first two steps must be made very fast. The second step should be as long as possible in order to effect a faked hand-off to the halfback. On completing the second step, the quarterback should drop his head and shoulders to complement the fake of the half-back's drive into the line.

The quarterback should try to come to a complete stop at the point of the hand-off fake. If he makes an uninterrupted move right on out to the defensive end, he will not give the end a chance to commit himself. The most successful maneuver is for the quarterback to take the first two steps very fast, come to a complete stop, then start up again to move on out to the end.

The next steps after the hand-off fake are for balance. The quarterback should straighten up and move his feet rapidly, taking short steps. He should watch the end relentlessly and run out to the end in an upright position, where he can move to his best advantage.

The ball is carried lightly at waist height. I believe

Fig. 51.

that bobbing the ball up and down has a tendency to relax the quarterback and to attract the attention of the defensive end, making it easier to fool him. Most important at this point is that the quarterback must not crouch, but must straighten up where he can see and move better.

The quarterback should try to force the end to play him. The toughest defender to work the ball past is the defensive end who merely stands flatfooted. If, as he shuffles his feet, the defensive end still has not committed himself, the quarterback should take a step up into the line, faking a keeper. This action will usually bring the defender in after him and the quarterback can lateral the ball off easily.

If the quarterback is going to keep, he should fake a lateral. If he is going to lateral, it will help to fake a keep by stepping up into the line. *If the quarterback is in doubt, he should always keep the ball.* He will never make a serious mistake by keeping the ball, since his path is on the line of scrimmage, where he will not lose any yardage. However, if the quarterback laterals when he should not, a great deal of yardage or even the ball may be lost.

When the quarterback keeps the ball, he should make certain that he cuts squarely up the field. A square corner and a straight-ahead drive up the field will give the quarterback his best opportunity to run, and will force the outside defenders to leave their territory to pursue him. After he has made his cut, the quarterback should be alert for the opportunity to lateral the ball out to the fullback or halfback. This lateral, it should be remembered, is not a blind throw but is made with his eyes on the receiver. A basketball-type of pass from the chest is suggested for this downfield lateral.

To make the lateral properly in the option area, the quarterback should drop the ball about 6 inches from its waist high position. At the same time, turn the hands so that the pitch may be made directly back to the halfback. The ball should leave off the tips of the quarterback's fingers. This method of releasing the ball gives him the best control of the lateral. The wrist action should give the ball a slight upward turn producing a soft throw. The target for the lateral should be the area between the halfback's waist and head.

The *fullback's* assignment on the option play is to move on a course 3 yards in front of the defensive end. He should run hard through this point and continue moving fast on an arc from his original position to a point 5 yards downfield.

The fullback should not block the defensive end unless he is on his path as he runs his arc. If the defensive end is inside of him, the fullback should pass him up and move on downfield to block the next defender. If this end is outside of him, he should shoulder him and turn up inside to block the halfback.

As the fullback encounters the secondary defenders, he should remember to run his course and not to turn inside to block defensive men. Only if the corner linebacker or defensive halfback crosses his arc should the fullback block. Otherwise, he stays right on his course and passes them up.

The *halfback* on the side where the play is being run should hit close to the quarterback as he fakes into the line. He should drive right on through the line to clear the way so that the quarterback can see the defensive end quickly. If he is successful in breaking through the line, then by running as if he were carrying the ball and faking well up the field, the halfback prevents the opposition from penetrating to the path of the quarterback. Good faking by this halfback will also pull the outside defenders to the inside, giving the play more chance of success.

The *halfback* on the side away from the play must assume a stance that gives the defense the impression he is going to run the straight-ahead hand-off. He must give no indication that he is going to break around to the opposite side on the snap.

The halfback must be certain that he is 5 yards deep as he reaches the lateral area. If the quarterback laterals the ball to him, the halfback should turn up the field quickly. If the quarterback keeps the ball through the lateral area, the halfback should cut sharply to put himself in position to take a downfield lateral.

Summary

Just as it is a good thing for the quarterback to have a check list, the remainder of the backfield can also do well in learning to check themselves in essentials necessary to move the ball effectively. High school players must be convinced that there is only one correct way of performing. Boys of this age have a tendency to accept a below-standard performance and will not adhere to the Split-T's exacting demands unless they are *sold* on the idea that careful attention to details will make them champions. Our high school players, I have found, will respond favorably to any task, however exhausting or unpleasant, if they are convinced it will raise them out of mediocrity. The immature players should be given a number of fundamentals that are essential to proper performance, and should be told that unless they pay them meticulous attention they may expect to be nothing but average players. This will usually strike a responsive chord, for high school players are ready to pay the price when they are certain it will make a difference.

Some of the points worthy of the backfield man's most careful attention are:

1. It is absolutely essential that our quarterback operate straight down the line of scrimmage, moving slightly forward as he approaches the end.
2. The halfbacks must come straight in to the same point on every hand-off play and must never look for the ball. Their eyes must relentlessly watch the blocking ahead and leave the responsibility of exchanging the ball to the quarterback. After receiving the ball, the halfback should make the proper cut and move in the proper direction.

3. It is necessary for the ball-carrier to be moving directly ahead at the exchange-point, giving no indication to which side of the defensive player he will go until the ball is in his possession.

4. When the halfbacks are faking the hand-off, they must always hit the proper hole. When he is not going to get the ball, the halfback should look at the ball. It is his responsibility to make a close mesh with the quarterback, since the quarterback is watching the defensive end. The halfback will almost certainly meet opposition as he goes through the line, but he must never flinch. Keep driving even if he is tackled.

5. It is imperative that the faking halfback hit quickly, so as to clear in front of the quarterback in time for him to see and react to the play of the defensive end.

6. The fullback must start for a spot 3 yards in front of the defensive end on all plays. By doing this, his faking will always be good.

7. The halfback from the far side coming around on the option play for the lateral must be 5 *yards* behind the line of scrimmage when he gets the ball. This will require some adjustment in depth after he starts, since his original position will be closer to the line of scrimmage.

8. The far halfback before he starts around on the option play must look as though he is going to run the hand-off. As he takes his stance, he should

have plenty of weight forward in order not to tip-off by his position the fact that the play is going to the opposite side.

9. The timing of the option play is adjusted to the fact that it will be necessary for the far halfback to start awkwardly and slowly, since his stance will not enable him to move laterally with ease. If the halfback *cheats* by pointing or jumping on his start, he will overrun the quarterback's lateral by reaching the option area too quickly.

10. The correct hand position for the halfbacks and the fullback when receiving the ball from the quarterback is: The outside hand is a little past the hip and a little under the shoulder with the wrist firmly pressed against the hip. The fingers should be spread and cupped slightly at the tips. The inside arm is bent at the elbow and carried very high. The wrist of the inside arm should be across the mouth of the ball-carrier, so the quarterback will not strike the back's elbow as he reaches for the pocket on the outside hip.

11. On the slant and option plays the quarterback should take his first two steps exactly as he does on the hand-off. He must give no indication that up to this point the play is not a hand-off. The second step should be very long just as it is on the hand-off. The long second step will bring the quarterback to a stop as he moves down the line and he should drop his head and shoulders at this

point, giving the defense the impression he is reaching for the halfback. However, the quarterback should not extend his hand to the halfback and keep the ball in close to his waist to prevent the ball's being knocked out of his hands by the faking halfback.

12. On the counter play, the second step of the quarterback should be very short. An attempt should be made to stop this foot even with the other foot on the second step. Unless he takes a short second step, the quarterback will have difficulty reaching the far hip of the fullback for a successful transfer of the ball.

13. The key to a successful slant play is to show the ball to the defensive end behind the fullback. This may be accomplished by swinging the ball back to arm's length in a fake lateral to the halfback. From this vantage point, the ball may be seen by the defensive end if the quarterback will allow the fullback to pass before pulling the ball back and stepping up to the line of scrimmage for the hand-off to the fullback. If the defender can see the ball behind the fullback, he is almost certain to move out to stop the wide play and leave the off-tackle position unprotected.

14. The halfbacks and the fullback must learn to run over the exchange point with short steps to increase their ability to cut sharply on the proper course.

15. The quarterback must actually look for the outside hip of the halfback on the hand-off. If he is unable to reach the hand-off pocket, he should keep the ball himself and follow the halfback into the line. Few fumbles will occur if the quarterback transfers the ball only when he is certain he can reach the far hip.

Operation of Backs and Ends on Pass Plays

THE SPLIT-T IS BASICALLY A RUNNING FOR-
mation. The offense can keep possession of the ball, make
first downs, and eventually score most consistently by
running with the ball. However, this fact becomes apparent to the defense and the opponents will overload
the line to stop the running attack. To face this type of
defense the Split-T must throw the ball.

Ironically, the team dedicated to running with the ball
often wins the game by passing. This happens because
the defense is waiting for the run and is caught unexpectedly by the pass. A point of offensive strategy is to do the
opposite of what the defense is expecting. However, to
realize any advantage from passing in the Split-T offense,
the team must first establish the threat of a run and,
second, have all passes develop after a running play
fake.

The passing attack of the Split-T is therefore developed after the initial movements have been made, exactly

as they are on a running play. The intent to pass is concealed as long as possible by good faking.

The Split-T lineman must fire out on pass plays just as he does on running plays. The offensive lineman provides the defense with its best key to pass plays. A secondary defender has only two things to look for that will tell him that the play will not be a pass. The offense cannot pass when the ball crosses the line of scrimmage. By clever ball-handling it may be difficult for the defenders to tell when the ball actually crosses the line of scrimmage. So the first and most reliable key to reveal the pass play is to watch for offensive linemen to cross the line. Most pass defenders key the offensive linemen for this reason.

The Split-T team cannot expect to catch the pass defenders unawares unless the linemen give no indication by their blocking that a pass is coming.

It should be remembered that the Split-T team is going to pass only when the defense overloads the line or commits their secondary defenders quickly, making the running plays ineffective. We are going to run with the ball until the defense assigns so many men to the line that they leave areas poorly protected against passes. This will cause the Split-T coaches to differ on several points with the coaches using other offensive formations. Our Split-T passing philosophy is based on the following principles:

First, no time will be spent trying to teach the pass receivers evasive tactics. Split-T receivers will merely run down the field cutting in or out with no fakes, hooks, stop and goes or other escape routines in his schedule.

Second, the offensive ends must fire out just as all other linemen do to hold their blocks for two counts before releasing to go for the pass. Since all pass plays start with a running play fake in which the end is a principal blocker, his initial steps must be exactly the same or the defense can tell the pass is coming.

Third, all backs must fake all the way through the line before releasing for the pass.

Fourth, all basic Split-T passes, except the counter pass, retain a run-pass option. On these passes with the running option, it is imperative that the passer run with the ball every time he can. Unless we run every opportunity we have, even though we can make only a few yards, we are seriously handicapping our ability to strike at a defensive weakness. To summarize the fundamentals of the Split-T passing attack we find:

1. We are going to stay basically on the ground. Make the first downs and we will score.
2. We will throw when the defense overloads the line stopping our running attack and leaving their secondary vulnerable to passes.
3. The initial steps of all pass plays will be identical to those of our running plays giving the defense no indication that a pass play is coming.
4. With good faking in the backfield and by holding the blocks of the offensive ends for two seconds, we will conceal the intent to pass until the last instant.
5. We will properly execute the pass-run option by

running with the ball every time we have an opportunity to make even a short gain.

The Counter Pass

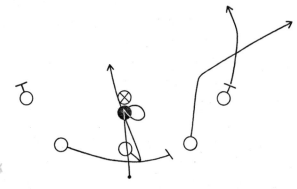

Fig. 52.

The quarterback starts his operation on the counter
pass by taking his first step up and out in the normal
manner. His second step is short and he makes a poor
fake to the halfback. A good fake to this halfback might
cause the defense to tackle the best potential receiver, so
the quarterback fakes poorly by holding the ball with
both hands near his body.

The third step completes the pivot and leaves the
quarterback facing directly toward his own goal. Squared
around with his feet in line and in an upright position
except for a quarter-bend at the knees, the quarterback
is ready for the fake with the fullback, who is still 2 yards
away.

As the fullback starts directly for the ball, the quarterback pops the ball out to place it in the fullback's stomach. The ball is thrust out at arm's length directly in front

of the quarterback's right hip, and is actually placed in contact with the fullback's stomach.

The fullback coming in forces the ball back into the quarterback's stomach. To avoid humping shoulders with the fullback as he drives by on the close mesh, which is necessary to get the most out of the fake, the quarterback steps up with his outside foot and drops his inside shoulder. The fullback should aim right at the ball and run right through the quarterback's lap.

The quarterback's right hand is behind the ball as he pops it out to the fullback and his left hand is over the end. This allows a large part of the ball to be placed in contact with the fullback's stomach and allows the left hand of the quarterback to be out of the way so that the fullback may clamp down on the right hand without the danger of tugging the ball away from the quarterback. As the fullback brings his arms down over the ball, the quarterback slides the ball out with his left hand and holds it in his stomach, while allowing the fullback to jerk his right hand slightly to accent the fake.

After the fullback has passed, the quarterback starts his move back to set up for the pass. He continues his fake as he drops leisurely back by allowing his right arm to follow the fullback and by watching the fullback as he drives into the line. The quarterback must gaze intently at the fullback if he is to make the defense believe that he has actually given the ball to him. The job may be performed better if the quarterback will pick out a spot somewhere on the fullback's back on which to fix his eyes.

The quarterback must not hurry as he drops back. It will take a lot of poise to move back slowly and ignore the rushing linemen, but his chances of reaching his throwing position are much better if he moves back leisurely.

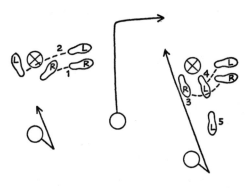

Fig. 53.

When the quarterback reaches a spot 6 yards behind the line of scrimmage, he should turn quickly and set up to pass. His two receivers are in the same area, so the passer does not have to scan the field. He can see immediately if the faking has worked and if one of the receivers is open. If neither of the receivers is open, the quarterback should bring the ball down and make a try to get back to the line of scrimmage as best he can. He should never throw when the receivers are covered, risking an interception. The yardage the quarterback will lose when he fails to make it back to the line of scrimmage will not hurt the offense nearly as much as the loss of the ball on an interception.

The *fullback* should line up a half-yard deeper than normal on the counter pass. This will give the defense an opportunity to see the fullback as he fakes and should lead them to expect a counter play. It is best for the fullback to make a more deliberate and slower movement on the pass than he does on the run. The timing of the play requires the fullback to hold his position until the quarterback has completed his pivot and has squared away facing him before he starts forward. He should be about 2 yards away when the quarterback has reached his faking position.

The fullback should run for the ball as the quarterback holds it out to him. He has the responsibility for the close mesh with the quarterback and the faking of the counter pass will not be effective unless he runs right over the ball.

His hand position will have the inside hand on his outside bicep. The other hand will be underneath the inside elbow. As the fullback approaches the quarterback, he should throw his inside elbow over the ball, clamping the quarterback's hand gently with his outside hand, which is under the elbow. This hand position will cause the fullback to lower his inside shoulder. When he folds his elbow over the ball he eliminates the possibility of striking the quarterback with his elbow as he passes.

The most important part of the fake is carried out by the fullback after he has passed the quarterback. He must drive into the line with his arms folded in the "rock-the-baby" style. If he will swing his arms back and forth in this manner, it will appear to the defensive team that he really has the ball. The fullback should drive forward until he is tackled.

The halfback on the side the play is being run will drive through the line just to the outside of the defensive tackle. If this halfback has been doing a good job of blocking on the defensive tackle on running plays, he should break through the line cleanly, for the defensive man will be happy to be rid of him.

Having cleared the line of scrimmage, the halfback breaks on one of two patterns. If the defense is three-deep he will cut toward the sideline in front of the defensive halfback, while the end, who is the other receiver, will cut out at 45 degrees trying to get behind the defensive halfback. If the opposing secondary is aligned in a box defense, the halfback cuts out at 45 degrees from a point 5 yards beyond the line of scrimmage and the end will run straight ahead looking for the ball over his inside shoulder.

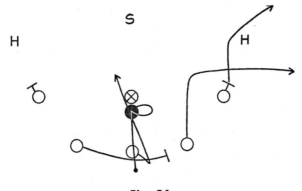

Fig. 54.

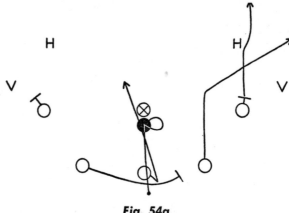

Fig. 54a.

The *halfback* from the opposite side is a blocker, but he must be careful not to move out beyond the position of the right guard as he comes around behind the fullback. It is best to stop quickly after passing the fullback in order to maintain an inside position from which to throw his block on the rushing end.

The end on the side away from the play will block. Like the remainder of the linemen, he must be certain that he does not give the pass away by any change of stance or manner of blocking that might differ from his normal procedure.

The Fullback Slant Pass

The quarterback's operation on the Fullback Slant Pass starts with his taking the first two steps normally. The first step is up and out and the second is a long step to the hand-off fake. However, the hand-off should be

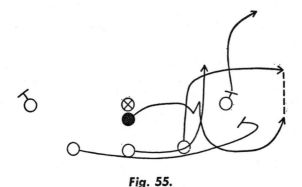

Fig. 55.

faked poorly to the halfback since he is again our number one receiver and we would not like to have him tackled.

The quarterback's third step is off the line about 18 inches and the fourth step brings the feet close together pointed away from the line of scrimmage at 45 degrees.

This position must be held until the fullback has passed. Since the fullback has the responsibility for coming in close for a good fake, the quarterback must come to a stop to avoid a collision. With his feet planted, he sticks the ball out to the fullback.

The ball should be placed in the fullback's stomach and should be held in this position until the fullback's forward motion drives the ball back to the quarterback. The quarterback pulls the ball out to place it on his hip and as the fullback drives by very close the quarterback drops his left foot back and rolls his body to face directly toward the sideline.

At this point it is important to remember that he is trying to hide the ball from the outside defenders. The quarterback should be careful not to show the ball to the defensive men in front of him as he moves away from the line of scrimmage to get depth. While taking a crossover and another step back, he should face the sideline with the ball behind him. Often at this point the quarterback will roll with the fullback as he goes by revealing the ball to the opponents. As the quarterback gains his depth away from the line of scrimmage with the two steps, he should gaze intently at the fullback to accent the fake. If the quarterback will really fix his eyes on some spot on the fullback's back, he will do a lot for his fake.

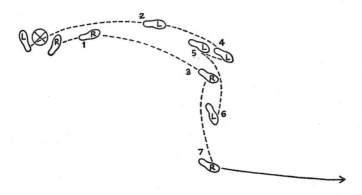

Fig. 56.

After the two quick steps watching the fullback, the quarterback makes his break to get outside. Now he should really take off. Running very fast, the quarterback brings the ball up to a passing position. Since we had rather he would run than throw the ball, we believe that by raising the ball quickly to a throwing position, the defense will move back to defend against a pass, giving the quarterback a better chance to run.

It can't be stressed too often that by running with the ball at every opportunity on these pass plays, the effectiveness of our offense can be greatly increased. It must be remembered that our objective is to make 4 yards a play, regardless of the play called, so if we can make a 4-yard gain by running with the ball on a pass play, we are doing well. Another point that has a bearing on this case is that the average high school team is able to complete only three of five passes thrown. This average holds even in practice, when running signals without a defense. On one of the five trials the passer will miss the receiver completely, and on another the receiver will drop the ball when it is right in his hands. So in a game when the defense is active, our chance of completing the pass is less than 50 per cent.

If the defensive secondary is closing in as the quarterback moves out around the end, he should throw the ball. To make his throw more effective, the quarterback should observe a very important point—he should turn up the field and be moving forward at the instant he releases the ball. This maneuver will make the pass much more accurate, especially when it is thrown while moving at top speed. It is very difficult to be accurate when making the pass while running parallel to the line of scrimmage. Turning up the field will aid in throwing more accurately and will place the quarterback in the best position to run with the ball.

The *fullback* on the slant pass should start in his usual

manner, running for a spot 3 yards in front of the defensive end on his first three steps. These steps should be shorter than his steps on the slant play, however, so that he cuts up toward the line of scrimmage nearer his original position by about a yard. Since the object of the fake is to make the defense think that he is taking the ball from the quarterback, the fullback should watch the quarterback from his first step.

The fullback has the responsibility for driving close to the quarterback to assure an effective fake, so he should watch the quarterback carefully to know when he is going to offer him the ball. When the quarterback plants his feet, the fullback should drive right at the ball.

The hand and arm positions for the fullback are the same as they were on the slant play. It is imperative that the ball actually be placed in the fullback's stomach so he must drive right through the quarterback's lap. The fake must be continued on through the line, with the fullback swinging his arms back and forth in the "rock-the-baby" style. This manner of faking may sound a little foolish and may look a bit peculiar as you try it for the first time, but I believe it is the best hand position to hide the fact that you do not have the ball. When the fullback is running hard with his arms folded in the manner described, he will give a realistic impression of a ball-carrier.

The *end* on the side where the play is being run will start his movement downfield by making a running shoulder block on the opponent in front of him. After he has hit the opponent for a full count, he releases him to run directly downfield to a point 8 yards beyond the line of scrimmage where he cuts out toward the sideline at 45 degrees.

The *on-side halfback* breaks on the count to drive just to the outside of the offensive tackle. When he breaks through the line, the halfback should cut 90 degrees toward the sideline. His pattern will carry him between 5 and 8 yards deep as he arrives in the territory where he may receive the pass from the quarterback.

The *halfback* from the opposite side has an important blocking role on the slant pass. He breaks around in his usual manner to set himself to block the defensive end. The halfback, who is aided materially by a good fake by the fullback, must block his man in. By breaking fast to the outside, the halfback may turn and set up on the defensive end while the defender is watching the fake. With the advantage of his outside position, the halfback can keep the defensive end from getting back out of the inside pocket if he goes for the fake at all.

The Swing Pass

The swing pass is the only reverse among the basic Split-T plays. The guards pull to lead the blocking for the quarterback as he sweeps wide around the end, away from the fake of the remainder of the backfield. Although this is the only play in which the linemen pull, they have plenty of time to get out in front of the ball-carrier before he starts in their direction after he has completed his fake and swings back to fall in behind the blockers. The time spent in faking allows the guards to fire out in the prescribed manner of pass blocking for split-T linemen and still pull ahead of the ball-carrier. This action makes the play hard to key by the defense.

The swing pass is an excellent running play, for the pulling guards give the quarterback an excellent opportunity of getting around the defensive end. The two ends

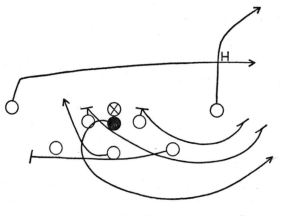

Fig. 57.

have plenty of time to run their pattern and force the secondary defenders back to protect against a pass, making it difficult for them to come up quickly to meet the runner. The ends are well located to apply turn-back blocks on the defenders if the quarterback decides to run to the outside. (See Figure 58.)

The run-pass option is retained on the swing pass. Unless the secondary defenders stay back with the offensive ends, a long pass has a good chance of getting behind them. However, as on the other running passes, we should run at every opportunity.

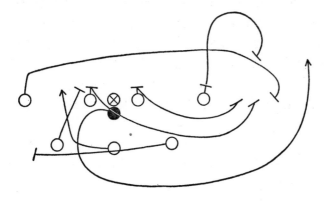

Fig. 58.

The *quarterback's* first step on the swing pass is out, but he does not step up. The second step is out and back, completing a pivot to bring the quarterback to the point where he sets up to meet the fake of the fullback.

The ball is thrust out to the fullback and is placed softly against his stomach as he comes in over it. The quarterback does not stop moving back as he steps up with his inside foot as the fullback pushes the ball back into his stomach.

Remembering that the people he is trying to fool are the defenders on the far side, the quarterback holds the ball in his stomach while rolling with the fullback. As he watches intently the faking fullback, the quarterback continues to move back, facing in the direction opposite to his intended run. When he reaches a point 5 yards behind the line of scrimmage, the quarterback drops his fake and really runs hard to get outside.

It is imperative that the quarterback move as fast as he can when he makes his break, for he is deep behind the line of scrimmage and must get to the outside to put the pressure on the defense with the run-pass option. After four or five hard steps at full speed, the quarterback brings the ball up to passing position. However, he must keep right on running to turn up the field. If he can see daylight, he merely continues to run. If the defensive secondary is closing in on him, the quarterback should throw the ball to one of the receivers who, under these conditions, should be in the open.

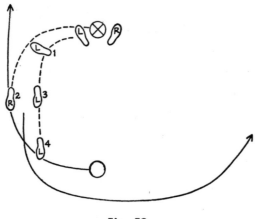

Fig. 59.

The *fullback* will take very short steps as he again fakes taking the ball from the quarterback to run the slant play. His path on the swing pass will be nearer the center than it was on the slant pass as he drives by the quarterback and on through the line just outside the offensive guard. However, the exact spot will be determined by the quarterback, who sets up the fake by thrusting the ball out to fix the target for the fullback.

The fullback will run directly for the ball with his arms in the position described for the counter pass and the slant pass. By standardizing the hand position of the fullback and the ball handling of the quarterback on all three pass plays, high school players may become proficient in faking. It will be noted that the quarterback is required to plant his feet and thrust the ball out gently, striking the fullback's stomach for actual contact on the counter pass, slant pass, and swing pass. The fullback drives straight for the ball and assumes the same hand position for his assignment for each of these plays. After a little practice the players will adjust their operations to each other for an excellent fake.

As with the other two pass plays, the fullback will execute his "rock-the-baby" swing with his arms to carry his fake well forward through the line. By faking hard as he nears the line of scrimmage, the fullback will often pick off shooting linemen or linebackers and prevent their penetration.

The *left halfback*, who is on the side where the fake is made, will drive into the line just outside of the left guard. This halfback's assignment is to block any lineman who might be trying to penetrate outside of this pulling guard. By working with the fullback, who is faking through the line just outside of him, the halfback can seal off the faking area until the quarterback has time to complete his fake and break out of the dangerous territory.

The *right halfback*, who is on the side away from the fake, will come around behind the fullback to block the defensive end. On the swing pass, this halfback will try to drive the defender directly out toward the sideline. It is best if the halfback can gain a slight inside position to drive the defensive end out and back with solid contact. Unless the halfback can stop this aggressive defender, he may catch the quarterback, who is delayed by his fake. Since the quarterback makes no attempt to hide the ball from this side of the line after the fullback has passed, the defensive end may spot the ball in the quarterback's stomach and try desperately to get to the ball-carrier. In this situation he must be blocked solidly.

I believe that hard blocking by the halfbacks is essential to success in the high school Split-T. A principal blocking role is assigned to one or more of the backfield men on each of the basic plays, so it would appear that a fast, elusive ball-carrier who doesn't like contact may not play well on the Split-T.

However, as a strong argument for our system of attack, I would like to point out that the Split-T player has the advantage of effectively faking before he blocks, thus putting the defender at a disadvantage.

Although I wish to make no attempt to draw a comparison between our formation and any other, I think a backfield man who is not aggressive is a handicap to any offense. For example, in an offensive formation that features the drop-back pass, there must be at least two backs who are willing to bear the punishment of hard-charging rushers. This, in my opinion, is rougher than backfield blocking in the Split-T.

As we finish our discussion of the swing pass, we are reminded that it is the last of this series of three Split-T passes that is based on the faking of the fullback and quarterback. The precise movement of the fullback as he drives by the quarterback holds the attention of the defense long enough for the receivers to maneuver into the open behind the distracted defenders. As has been mentioned previously, the manner of faking by the quarterback and the hand position of the fullback have been standardized, making it necessary for these two players to learn only one operation for all three plays. This advantage allows time for the players, by working carefully, to perfect their fake to the point where they can convince the defense that the ball has actually been handed-off to the fullback.

The two remaining basic Split-T passes do not depend on a fake to the fullback. The option pass is, of course, the option play with receivers down the field to add a run-pass option. The quick pass is based on a quick pitch by the quarterback to the halfback, who races out around the end where he has a choice of running or passing.

The option pass actually has two options. The quarterback may keep the ball and run with it himself or he may lateral it back to the halfback. The halfback, once the ball is in his possession, may either run or pass.

The Option Pass

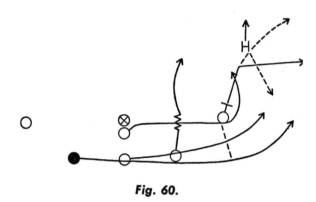

Fig. 60.

The *quarterback's* operation is almost identical to his maneuver on the option play. His first step is up and out; his second step is long for the hand-off fake to the halfback. His next steps are for balance as he straightens up to a position where he can see the end and try to move the ball by the defender. The quarterback must remember the defensive end can force him to keep the ball on this pass just as he can on the option play. If he can lateral the ball off to the halfback, the quarterback should try to get in the blocking ahead of the play.

The on-side halfback drives into the line just outside of the offensive tackle. His first responsibility is to seal off the territory outside the tackle, so as he nears this area the halfback should slow up. Since the end is the number one receiver on this play, he will execute a running shoulder block on the opponent in front of him and move quickly downfield. This means that the halfback should remain in the hole inside the end until the quarterback has passed his position. After he has closed off the area against penetration by the defense, the halfback will break down the middle straight ahead of his original position. He will not be able to go deep because he has been delayed by his blocking assignment, but occasionally this halfback will be open for a pass because the defenders moved away as he was slowly coming through the line.

The *fullback* moves off on his normal course headed for a spot 3 yards in front of the defensive end. If the defensive end is inside of him as he runs his arc, the fullback passes him up to block the next defender. However, if the defensive end is outside his path, the fullback should block him. The fullback must move quickly out to his blocking assignment in order not to delay the ball-carrier if he should decide to run on the play.

The *halfback* from the side away from the play should come around just as he does on the option play. When he receives the lateral, the halfback should not hesitate but should continue to run hard to the outside and make his turn up the field where he executes his run-pass option. The halfback should run every time that he can make any yardage, but if the defense is closing in on him, he should throw the ball. He should never run laterally across the field and try to throw the ball while on this course. A much more accurate throw will result if the halfback will make his turn up the field and deliver the ball while running toward the line of scrimmage.

The *end* on the side where the play is being run should

shoulder block the man in front of him. He should hit this man with a running shoulder block and hold the block as long as he can. My experience has shown that when the end tries to hold the defender as long as he can with a straight-shoulder block, he is never able to keep contact longer than 2 seconds. He will not be delayed too long if he tries to hold his contact as long as he can. By executing a regular shoulder block, the end conceals the pass better and increases his chances of getting open for the pass.

After executing his blocking assignment, the end runs directly toward the defensive halfback. The action of the defensive halfback will determine what the end does on the play. If he drops back in pass defense, the end cuts toward the side line at 90 degrees. If the halfback is moving up to reinforce the line when the end releases his block, the end should go deep and cut out at 45 degrees. The former action will put the end in the best blocking position if the halfback decides to run with the ball, for the ball-carrier will likely keep right on going when he sees that the defensive halfback is back to defend against the pass. In this case, the end will be in front of the defender where he can block for the runner. The halfback will likely see little opportunity to run with the ball when the defensive halfback comes rushing up to reinforce the outside and will be ready to throw. In this case, the end will be downfield ready to receive the pass.

The Quick Pass

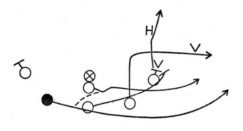

Fig. 61.

The quick pass should be called when the defense has a man playing on the offensive end with the secondary in a box defensive alignment. This is a common defense against the Split-T, since most 5-4 and 6-3 defenses use

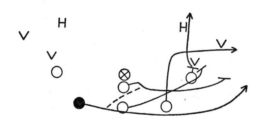

Fig. 62.

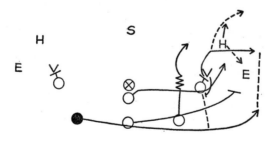

Fig. 62a.

this alignment. The three-deep defense that has a defensive end on the line of scrimmage outside the offensive end may be attacked more effectively with the option pass.

The quick pass takes advantage of the defensive alignment in which the defender is playing in front of the end, by having the offensive player block him before going downfield for a pass. This holds the defensive man in position until the fullback has time to arrive and throw the clinching block on him. This maneuver is necessary for the success of the play. (Naturally, the end can't block a defensive player who is lined up several yards outside of him in order to set him up for the fullback's clean-up block.) So the quick pass is only recommended for box secondary defenses.

The *quarterback's* successful operation on the quick pass is dependent on his ability to get the lateral off to the halfback quickly and to hurry out to lead the ball-carrier around the end. He should pivot as soon as his foot on his first step strikes the ground and, twisting his body around, pitch the ball to the halfback. The lateral should be made with one hand and delivered so quickly that the halfback will still be in the process of taking his first step, and will be at least 2 yards behind the quarterback.

After lateralling the ball, the quarterback should move at top speed behind the fullback in order to be in position to block the corner linebacker. It is essential for the quarterback to give ground away from the line of scrimmage to avoid bumping into the fullback, but it is best to move as close to the line as possible. Staying close to the line of scrimmage not only allows the quarterback to get out faster, but it puts him in the best position to block the corner linebacker if he rushes across the line of scrimmage to put pressure on the halfback. The most successful play often occurs when the offensive end and fullback can knock the defensive end off his feet and the quarterback drives the corner linebacker wide, thus allowing the ball-carrier to cut up the field inside of him. (Note Figure 63.)

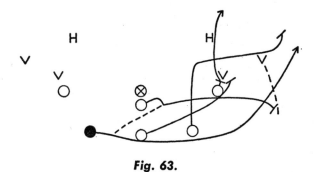

Fig. 63.

If the corner linebacker is dropping back into pass defense when the quarterback arrives, he should cut up the field to lead the play.

On the quick pass the *fullback* starts quickly and runs at top speed directly for a point 1 yard outside the offensive end. He will have the help of a strong block by the end before this player goes downfield as a pass receiver, but the fullback must accept the full responsibility for preventing the defensive end from moving laterally into the path of the ball-carrier. The fullback must realize that the play has little chance for success unless the defensive end is cut down. Once this defender is knocked off his feet, the offense has gained control of the situation. For no matter what the corner linebacker may do, he is always wrong. If the corner man rushes the ball-carrier, he is an easy target for the block of the quarterback and he leaves the on-side halfback wide open for a short pass behind him. If this corner linebacker falls off to protect against the pass, the halfback will run with the ball with the quarterback leading him.

The key to success with the quick pass lies in the fact that the combined blocking by the end and the fullback must prevent the defensive end from getting in the area of the run-pass option.

The *halfback* on the side where the play is directed should drive quickly through the line and cut out toward the sideline at 90 degrees. This halfback has no blocking duties on the quick pass as he does on the option pass, so he should clear the line quickly to reach his receiving area ahead of the ball-carrier. He can recognize the situation immediately, for if the corner linebacker is not protecting his territory, he will be open for a pass. If, however, the corner man is back covering him, the halfback should get in the best position to help with the blocking, for the play will be a run.

The *halfback* from the opposite side should look for the ball as he takes his first step. Once he has possession of the ball the halfback should run at top speed. It is definitely a mistake for this halfback to raise the ball and threaten to pass before he has reached the position of the offensive end on the far side. This will cause the pursuing linemen to move quickly to congest the territory ahead of him. He should race around the end and make his turn up the field before he considers his run-pass option. If the halfback will move at top speed to reach this point, the decision to run or pass will not be difficult. He keeps right on going unless the defense is closing in on him.

The *on-side end* performs his most important function on the quick pass in his first move by throwing a hard-shoulder block into the defender in front of him. As has been explained, he must block this defensive man to the best of his ability before he moves out for the pass. To carry out his assignment properly, the end should block the defender and hold his contact as long as possible. When the defender frees himself, the end moves straight-ahead quickly, looking over his outside shoulder for the pass.

Special Plays
and Their Use

IF THE HIGH SCHOOL TEAM HAS BEEN SUC-
cessful in moving the ball well, they may expect their
opponents to present some unorthodox defensive alignments. The opponents will practice hard against the basic
plays of the Split-T and will try to break down the splits
of the linemen and confuse the blocking assignments of
the offense. The defensive linemen can be expected to
stunt, and by cross-charging, looping, and sliding they
hope to reach the quarterback as he moves down the line
of scrimmage, thus forcing a fumble. Such tactics may
prevent the offense from moving the ball well at the out-
set of the game, and may upset the attacking team mentally. For this reason, I advocate using special plays as
the most effective method of retaliating against the stunting tactics of the defense.

To be successful, the opponents must have scouted the
offense well. They must be able to key the maneuvers of
the offensive players quickly in order to move rapidly

enough to stop the attack. The principal purpose of the special plays will be to capitalize on the tendency of the defensive team to overplay these keys.

As a point of strategy, I think the offensive team should start the game with the specials. These new plays will show the defense something that they have not seen in their scout report and for which they could have no pre-game plans. We hope to force the defense to make adjustments on the field to meet our specials, and therefore lose their poise in meeting our regular attack when we return to it. We should run our specials often until the defense makes their adjustments to them. As soon as the defensive team successfully meets the new attack, we should base our offense on our normal pattern. Unless the opponents are seasoned players, they will lose some of their confidence and will not be as sharp in stopping the basic plays after this experience.

The most unusual and weird patterns may be used as specials provided they are not used in consecutive games. The most extreme alignments would be best if used only once a season. However, even when a special is used only once they will help the offense for the remainder of the season. The scouts for future opponents can't ignore the plays for fear they might be repeated against his team. An opponent who is played in the last half of the season may have accumulated a number of these specials that will require a lot of time if a defense is prepared for each of them.

The special plays will help the offense retain the initiative. They will also help to keep the opponents playing carefully in order to defend his territory honestly. The defender will not be able to dash off to the point of attack when he sees a key, since a trap or reverse may strike at the area he has left unprotected. For this reason the specials are more valuable in helping the basic plays move the ball well than they are for the yardage they actually gain. They make a real contribution to the offense if they force the defense to play in a normal pattern. The basic Split-T plays will move the ball against orthodox defenses.

Any play from any formation may be used in conjunction with the Split-T as a special play. Plays from the Single Wing, Double Wing, Spread Formation and all others are now being used by college teams for the purpose of upsetting the defense. However, we will discuss only a few plays from the standpoint of trying to counter the unusual movements of the defense and use these movements to an offensive advantage.

Our specials will fall into three categories: *traps,* which are designed to take advantage of aggressive defensive linemen trying to penetrate; *reverses,* that strike in the opposite direction from the pursuit of defenders who key too quickly; and *particular plays* that strike at the weakness of a particular defense. The particular plays are called *automatics* since the quarterback may make the automatic call from the line of scrimmage, changing the play that he called in the huddle.

Traps

The basic plays of the Split-T hit straight ahead with a great deal of pressure, so the defense will often commit their linemen aggressively to meet this pressure. Since there are no traps among the basic plays of the Split-T, traps have been added to the special plays to take advantage of these penetrating linemen.

The Split-T with its shuffling quarterback and split line is a very poor passing formation when the defense knows it is going to pass. For this reason, it is usually better to call a trap instead of a pass on a long yardage situation. One of the most successful of all Split-T specials is the End Trap, which develops off the fake of the Swing Pass.

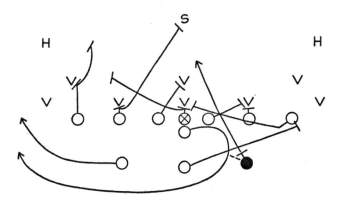

Fig. 64.

The End Trap. The left end should block the man in front of him in his usual manner, but he should release his contact quickly to move on down the field and block the halfback.

The left tackle will also make a hard straight-ahead block on the defender in front of him and hurry out to block the safety man.

The left guard will block the middle linebacker. This blocker will find his task easier if he will try to hold his contact and merely take the linebacker the way the defensive man wants to go.

The center on snapping the ball will make a hard block on the middle guard. Since the center's first responsibility is to set this man up for the trap, he should hit the defender with his right shoulder. This should give an alert defensive player the impression the center is trying to move him to the right. The middle guard's natural reaction would be to move to his left, which will take him away from the point of attack. After his initial move, the center releases quickly to pick up the block on the linebacker, who has been momentarily blocked by the left end.

The right guard will double-team with the right tackle to drive the lineman in front of the tackle away from the path of the ball-carrier. The two offensive linemen should try to move the defensive man laterally down the line toward the sideline. Driving the defender off the line of scrimmage will give him a chance to roll out of the block and catch the delayed trap play before the ball-carrier can cross the line of scrimmage.

The right end, who is the trapper on the play, should start by dropping his left foot back off the line about 6 inches. From this point, the end moves in a straight line to a point one foot behind the middle guard. This action of directing his block to come up behind the defensive man will give the end an opportunity to drive the guard out and back. A trap block is much easier to com-

plete successfully if the trapper will gain this advantage
in position. The trapper fails most often when he allows
the defensive player to step back off the line of scrimmage and move to the play before it has gained more
than a yard. Penetration across the line by the defensive
man will be to the trapper's advantage, since it will carry
him away from the play.

The quarterback on the End Trap will start his move
exactly as he does on the Swing Pass. As he comes around,
the quarterback should fake giving the ball to the fullback. However, as the fullback is running a path that is
wider than his course on the Swing Pass, the quarterback will not be able to fake the hand-off as effectively.
The quarterback moves back as deep as the right halfback to make his turn for the opposite sideline. At this
point, and just as he is making his turn, the pitch is made
to the waiting right halfback. The ball should be released
from the quarterback's hand 6 inches from the ground
and should be caught by the halfback at this height. If
the pitch is low, the defense will be unable to see the
ball from across the line of scrimmage. The quarterback,
after pitching the ball to the halfback, carries out his
fake by running hard around the end and by never looking back to see if the throw is caught.

The fullback runs a straight line for the outside foot of
the offensive right end. He makes the best fake that he
can while staying on this wide course as he passes the
quarterback. The fullback's path will take him in front of
the halfback, who is waiting for the ball, and will help
to hide this ball-carrier from the defense. His final re-

sponsibility requires the fullback to pick off any defender who sizes up the play and tries to follow the trapping end down the line.

The right halfback is the ball-carrier. As the ball is snapped, the halfback takes a quarter-turn to face the original position of the fullback. Here he waits for the ball by remaining very low and forming a pocket to receive the pitch with his hands at shoe-top height. The halfback must be certain to field the ball and have complete control of it before he starts forward. The timing of the play will permit him to wait on the ball and still receive the full advantage of the blocking.

The left halfback fakes wide around the left end, trying to gain and hold the attention of the defensive halfback until the downfield blocking can set up to hit him.

Since the End Trap is executed off the Swing Pass Fake, it makes an excellent play for a third-down-and-eight situation. The defense will expect a pass; the secondary will be deeper than normal, so that they can't recover as quickly; and the linemen will rush hard, making them more susceptible to trap blocking.

The Quick Cutback.   The Quick Cutback is a trap designed to work well on the defensive team that is keying the initial movements of the players on the Quick Pass. The Cutback that looks like the Quick Pass in its first steps should take advantage of a tendency by the defense to pursue the wide play too quickly. If the defense leaves the middle of the line poorly protected by moving rapidly to reach the anticipated point of attack of the wide

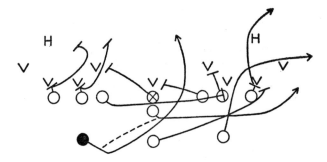

Fig. 65.

play, this trap in the center of the line has an excellent chance of being successful.

The left end blocks the man in front of him solidly, but releases him quickly to move downfield to block the defensive halfback. Since the halfback will likely move quickly with the flow of the play, the end should remember to lead him by 4 or 5 yards in order to be certain to cut him off.

The left tackle is assigned to block the defensive halfback on the other side of the field. Since the tackle must move at top speed to cross the path of the ball-carrier before the play develops, he must hit the player in front of him and move out rapidly. If the tackle can arrive in time to get to the halfback ahead of the ball, the blocking assignment is easy. The defensive halfback should be pulled out of position by the fake of the Quick Pass, making him an easy target.

The left guard is the trapper. He pulls out of the line by stepping back with his right foot and moves between the center and the quarterback to block the first defender outside the offensive tackle. The guard should anticipate meeting his opponent in the toughest position by directing his charge at a point one foot behind the defensive man. This action gives the trapper an excellent chance of completing his assignment successfully.

The center and the right guard will use a double-team block to move the middle guard away from the play. The blockers must be careful that they move the defensive guard laterally and not drive him back off the line. To do so will give him a chance to get back into the play before the ball-carrier can break past.

The right tackle brushes inside the defensive man in front of him to block the linebacker. This linebacker may be moving to the outside if he has taken the fake of the Quick Pass, so the tackle may best perform his assignment on him by maintaining his contact and going in the direction he wants to go.

The right end's principal responsibility is to give the defensive team the impression that the Quick Pass is coming. He must make his movements identical to his action on the Quick Pass by blocking the lineman in front of him solidly, allowing the fullback to take over, before he moves on downfield to run his pattern as a pass receiver.

The quarterback pivots on his first step to flip the ball back to the left halfback just as he does on the Quick Pass, and runs hard to the outside to carry his fake well up the field. By faking well, the quarterback will lead the secondary to revolve up to the outside too wide to stop the Cutback.

The fullback also follows the exact steps of his action on the Quick Pass. He should carry his fake through by setting up to block the defensive end as this defender is released by the offensive end.

The left halfback steps laterally with his right foot on the snap. He straightens up slightly at this point and waits for the lateral from the quarterback. After the halfback has the ball in his possession, he drives hard over the position of the right guard.

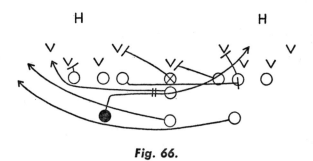

Fig. 66.

The Cross-Buck. Our last trap is the Cross-Buck. This play is most effective against a defense that moves laterally to stop the Hand-off Play. The Cross-Buck gives the offense a fine change of pace and will gain consistently if the defense is pursuing too rapidly.

The ends make their normal block on the opposing linemen before hurrying to a downfield assignment of blocking the defensive halfbacks.

The tackles, guards, and center will have the same assignment on the Cross-Buck as they have on the Cutback. These interior linemen open the path for the ball-carrier with a trap up the middle that is identical to the trap on the Cutback.

The quarterback fakes the Hand-off Play on the Cross-Buck but he will be unable to step up and out on his first step since the trapping guard must pass between him and the center. He moves out and off the line slightly as he transfers the ball to his left hand to make the hand-off. After placing the ball in the pocket on the right hip of the halfback, the quarterback continues out to the defensive end and cuts up the field just as he does on the hand-off.

The right halfback and the fullback run through the same maneuver they use on the Hand-off Play.

The left halfback takes his first step straight ahead but cuts sharply from this point to allow the quarterback to move between him and the line of scrimmage. The half-back takes the ball with his hands, forming a pocket on the opposite side from the usual one in taking the ball on the hand-off. With the ball firmly in his grip, the half-back cuts over the original position of the right guard.

Reverses

Since the defensive teams have adapted the hit-and-slide type of maneuver that enables the players along the line to pursue the ball-carrier quickly, the Split-T attack has needed an effective reverse play. To be successful, the reverse must have its initial movements exactly the same as the normal pattern of the basic plays. The defense must be led to believe that the reverse play is faithfully following the continuity of the straight-ahead attack so that they will start their move on an angle of pursuit. Once the defense moves for three or four steps in the wrong direction, the offense will receive the full advantage of the reverse play.

Since the players must be convincing in their initial moves to deceive the opponents into moving in the wrong direction, the reverse plays develop slowly.

For this reason the play is not always successful and must be used carefully. However, I think that the real value of reverse plays may not be measured by the yardage gained by the reverses, but in keeping the defensive alignment honest and preventing the defense from pursuing so rapidly that it stops the regular attack. Reverse plays should be used regularly to balance the offensive attack even when the yardage they gain is not sensational.

The Quick Reverse. A popular defensive maneuver that is designed to stop the Quick Pass is to revolve the secondary quickly toward the flow of the play on the center snap. Since a basic move on the Quick Pass is for the right end to block the defender in front of him until the fullback can arrive to take the assignment over, the end is delayed too long to break away from the defensive halfback from the opposite side. Note in Figure 67 that the defensive maneuver is effective against the Quick Pass.

The Quick Reverse was developed to counter the revolving secondary. When the defense keys the initial movements of the Quick Pass, the Quick Reverse becomes an attractive play. The Reverse starts the defense off rap-

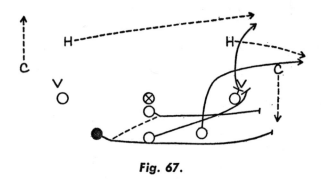

Fig. 67.

idly in the wrong direction by observing with absolute
fidelity the first steps of the Quick Pass.

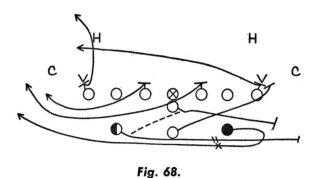

Fig. 68.

The left end blocks the defender in front of him to
start his assignment in the normal manner. Releasing
quickly, the end runs a pattern that takes him deep.
He should move as straight down the field as he can and
still be in position to look for the ball over his outside
shoulder.

The tackles execute their normal pass protection block

by striking out and dropping back low to hit out again. With this action, the tackles will duplicate their assignment on the Quick Pass.

The guards will pull out of the line and lead the ball-carrier just as they do on the Swing Pass. They must be certain to strike out before pulling in order to confuse the defense if they happen to be keying the offensive linemen. This blocking in the line will delay the guards long enough for the backfield to move out of their path and will help the timing of their blocking. If the guards should pull out too quickly, they would arrive at a point behind the left end ready to turn up the field too far ahead of the ball-carrier. The ball-carrier must fake well to the opposite side before turning back.

The center performs his normal pass protection block after snapping the ball.

The right end should block the man in front of him just as he does on the Quick Pass. The end will make his fake more effective if he will hold his contact with the defensive man until the fullback can take over to pick up the block. Since the defense will likely watch the end carefully for this key to the play, the end should faithfully execute his maneuver exactly as he does on the Quick Pass. The end's pass pattern has him cutting across the field rather shallow toward the original position of the defensive halfback.

The quarterback accepts the ball from the center and makes his quick pitch to the halfback. His next move is to hurry out to the outside position where he will contribute to the fake. The quarterback should block any defender that tries to follow the reversing halfback as he turns to take the ball.

The fullback's operation on the Quick Reverse is identical to his maneuver on the Quick Pass, so his foremost responsibility is to fake well. He drives for a point a yard to the outside of the offensive end to pick up the defender just as he is released by the end. The fullback should carry this assignment through for the best results.

The left halfback takes the lateral from the quarterback on his first step and starts his course to the opposite side of the field just as he does on the Quick Pass. After the right halfback has made his reverse turn and has started back, the left halfback should hand the ball off to his teammate and continue his fake well around the right end.

The right halfback should start by moving laterally toward the sideline. On his third step, the halfback should make his turn and complete his reverse to take the ball while moving to the opposite side. The hand-off should be made about a yard behind the halfback's original position. After receiving the ball, the halfback's assignment is the same concerning the run-pass option as it is on the Quick Pass. If the defense revolved away from him, he should follow the guards out around the end and continue to run with the ball. However, if the defense has recovered from the faking and is closing in on him, the halfback should throw the ball to one of the ends who, under these conditions, is almost certain to be open.

The Shield Reverse. The Shield Reverse is designed to counter a move by the defense that hampers the

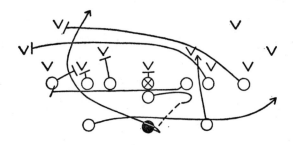

Fig. 69.

Option Play. The defensive team has been coached to expect the Option Play when the end passes up the defender in front of him to block the next man to his inside. This is a very accurate key, since the only time the end executes this type of blocking on any of the basic plays is on the Option Play.

Many defensive teams key the offensive halfbacks. When one of the halfbacks dives into the line and the other one starts his normal course to the opposite side, the defense moves quickly in that direction. If the opponents are using this key, the Shield Reverse will catch them off balance. This play has the normal movement of the halfbacks to the strong side, so that the defense can be effectively led away from the path of the ball-carrier by the reverse.

The Shield Reverse receives its name from the action of the halfback moving in front of the fullback to shield his counter step from the defensive linemen. This action permits the fullback to reverse his movement to run opposite to the flow of the play without being immediately detected by his opponents.

The left end helps the left tackle with a double-team block on the defensive man in front of the tackle. The offensive blockers should be careful to prevent the defender from rolling out, for the play is slower than normal in reaching the point of attack.

The left guard and center execute their normal block by firing out to engage the opponent across the line of scrimmage ahead of them with a straight-shoulder block.

The right guard pulls after faking a pass protection block on the linebacker. This fake helps to conceal the Reverse Play and keeps the guard up on the line of scrimmage so the quarterback will not be hampered as he moves down the line behind him. After the blocker pulls, he should be cautious to stay close to the line of scrimmage trying to gain an inside position on the first defensive man outside the offensive end. Contact with the defender should be made with the guard's head to the inside, in order to drive the opponent out and back away from the path of the ball-carrier.

I feel that pulling the guard from the side of the line away from the play makes the reverse far more effective than pulling the guard nearest the point of attack. In this case the right guard is farther away from the path of the ball-carrier and will arrive just ahead of the fullback, making his assignment easier. With this timing, to allow the runner to break through, it will be necessary for the guard to hold his contact with the defensive end for only a short time.

Another advantage to pulling the far guard is that the linebacker will often follow a pulling lineman. When a linebacker is keying the right guard on this reverse, he will find his angle of pursuit difficult. The linemen on the left side are blocking straight ahead and the sliding linebacker will find his path congested as he tries to follow the pulling guard. Notice in Figure 70 how easy it is for the linebacker to follow the near guard when he pulls.

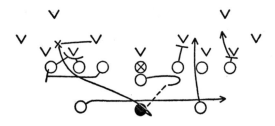

Fig. 70.

The right tackle and right end move sharply to their inside to give the defense the impression that the Option Play is coming to the right side. This move starts the tackle and end in the direction of their downfield assignment, which is to reach the outside defenders across the field. If these linemen go as much as 5 yards deep behind the line of scrimmage, they will be unable to reach their blocks ahead of the fullback with the ball. By taking a shallow course and running hard, the end and tackle help the runner break away for a long gain if he clears the line of scrimmage.

The quarterback moves out in his normal manner

through his first two steps to make a hand-off fake to the halfback. At this point the quarterback comes to a stop, just as he does on the Counter Play. By planting his feet on a line, he pivots quickly to face the fullback. From this position the quarterback laterals the ball to the fullback, making an effort to keep the ball low in order to hide it more effectively from the defensive linemen. After the lateral, the quarterback completes his fake by running on out around the right end.

The right halfback fakes on the Shield Reverse by driving straight ahead into the line. Since the offense is trying to carry out the initial movements of the Option Play, the halfback should pattern his maneuver after his operation on the Option. He may expect to find his path a little rough, for the offensive linemen in front of him are releasing their blocks quickly to hurry to their downfield assignments. The defensive linemen are almost certain to hit the halfback hard, but by faking hard he can cut off some of the pursuit of the defensive team.

The left halfback chooses a path a little closer to the line of scrimmage than normal as he moves across to the right side. His principal duty on the play is to shield the fullback (while the latter is taking his counter step) from the defense by running between the ball-carrier and the line of scrimmage. The halfback should carry his fake well around the end and up the field, attempting to hold the attention of the defensive players in that area as long as possible.

The fullback should line up a half-yard deeper than normal on the Shield Reverse. As the ball is snapped, the fullback should execute the counter step just as he does on the Counter Play. By holding the fake a little longer than he does on the Counter Play, the fullback will allow the left halfback to clear in front of him and give the quarterback time to make his fake and his pivot. After completing his fake, the fullback faces the quarterback and waits for his lateral by forming a pocket with his hands at shoe-top height. When he has control of the ball, the fullback heads for the hole. If he is successful in breaking through the line, he should cut toward the middle of the field looking for his downfield blockers coming across.

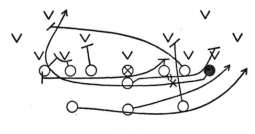

Fig. 71.

The End Around. The third reverse is the End Around, which may be run with the same blocking in the line as the Shield Reverse.

The high school coach will find the End Around a very effective reverse if he has an end who is a capable ball-carrier. However, if neither of the ends is effective carrying the ball, the coach may prefer to rely on the Shield Reverse in order for the ball to be handled by the backfield. There are some attractive features to the

End Around that should be considered. It is easier to hide the ball on the End Around, since the entire backfield is running their normal pattern to the right. It is difficult to see the hand-off to the end. The latter passes between the fullback and the quarterback, and the defense may revolve toward the expected point of attack only to find they have moved away from the path of the reverse.

The offensive line, with the exception of the right end, will block exactly as they do on the Shield Reverse. On the snap, the right end will step back with his inside foot and move behind the line of scrimmage to a point about a yard deep to the opposite side. As he approaches the quarterback, the end should assume the accepted hand position of the halfbacks on a hand-off play. After receiving the ball, the end should follow the pulling guard closely to cut inside his block and cut up the field.

The quarterback on the End Around takes his usual steps down the line of scrimmage, but as he does so, he should shift the ball to his right hand quickly. Continuing on his path close to the line, the quarterback should hand the ball off to the end and carry his fake downfield by running hard.

The right halfback, for his assignment on the End Around, duplicates his action on the Option Play.

The fullback should move on his normal course, except that on this play he should aim for a point only a yard in front of the defensive end. If the defensive end tries to follow the end as he pulls behind the line, the fullback should shoulder him before moving on up the field. This defender will not be able to catch the end after the hand-off, for the quarterback will cut off his pursuit. So the fullback need only to brush him to prevent him from hampering the hand-off.

The left halfback executes his fake around the opposite end and up the field, just as he does on the hand-off.

The Automatics

The Automatics are special plays that are called from the line of scrimmage by the quarterback. This call automatically checks the play called by the quarterback in the huddle and replaces it with the new play called on the line of scrimmage. The Automatics are particular plays for particular defenses. When the quarterback recognizes a particular defense after the team has lined up on the ball, he makes the automatic call that checks the signals previously given and switches it to the particular play that hits the weakness.

The quarterback is instructed to base his offense on the Automatics when he sees one of the particular defenses. Since the special plays are usually far more effective against this defense, the Automatic should be used three or four plays when the defensive team is aligned in this manner. However, the objective of the offense should be to run the defense out of the unorthodox alignment, so that the normal pattern for attack may be used.

The classic example of this type of special play is the Quick Pitch to the fullback when the opponents are defending against the Split-T with a stunting 4-4 defense. The 4-4 defense reaches the ultimate in cross-charging by committing all eight of the linemen and linebackers on a different pattern each down. This confusing maneuver can make it difficult to move the ball with any certainty when using only the basic plays. However, when all eight of these defensive players are trying to penetrate, they leave the outside vulnerable to the Quick Pitch. This Automatic will often catch the defense so unexpectedly that the fullback will break all the way to the defensive halfback without meeting any opposition.

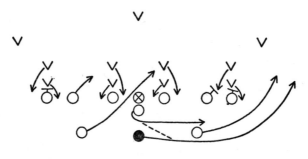

Fig. 72.

The Quick Pitch. On the Quick Pitch, the ends try to block the defensive men in front of them. If the ends can make a solid contact on these defenders, they can keep them from reaching the play.

The tackles should try to block the linebackers in the direction of the play. If this linebacker's stunt is shooting to the inside, the tackle meets him before he can penetrate. If the linebacker is shooting to the outside, the tackle should run through his original position and try to get downfield quickly enough to lead the ball-carrier.

The guards also try to make solid contact with the men aligned in front of them. However, penetration by the defense in this area is not likely to hamper the offense, since the quarterback rolls back off the line to make his lateral to the fullback. The fake up the middle by the left halfback tends to freeze the defense at this point and delays any pursuit.

The center has the same assignment as the tackles, since he tries to block the linebacker nearest him in the direction of the play. If this linebacker is shooting the gap away from him, the center should run hard on a shallow path and try to get in front of the ball-carrier.

The quarterback should follow the charge of the center far enough to get the ball. His next move after receiving the ball is to pivot on his right foot to make a fake hand-off to the left halfback. On completing his turn, the quarterback pitches the ball to the fullback, giving him plenty of lead to enable him to speed around the end without delay.

On the snap, the right halfback flares out toward the sideline to place himself in the best position for leading the fullback to the outside.

The left halfback has the assignment of faking up the middle.

The fullback pivots when the ball is snapped and runs slowly, getting a yard or two deeper before receiving the lateral from the quarterback. Once the ball is in his possession, the fullback should run wide to the outside at top speed.

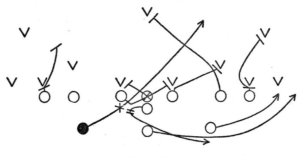

Fig. 73.

The Quick Trap. Another Automatic that hits the weakness of a particular defense is the Quick Trap. Using the same backfield maneuver as the Quick Pitch, the Quick Trap is unusually effective against an even defensive alignment without a middle linebacker.

The wide-tackle-six and the eight-man-line are two of the most common defenses that are weak against the Quick Trap. The cross-charge works well on the eight-man-line because it has no linebackers; on the wide-tackle-six the linebackers are too wide to reinforce the middle.

The Quick Trap should be used as an Automatic, so the quarterback may call it from the line of scrimmage to hit the weakness of the defense.

The ends should block the man in front for a full count before releasing quickly to move downfield for a block on the defensive halfback. Anticipating that the defensive halfbacks will close quickly to the middle once they recognize the trap, the ends should lead the secondary defenders by 4 or 5 yards. This action may give the ends the opportunity to help clear the middle for the path of the ball-carrier.

The tackles take a normal charge at the linebackers in front of them. The right tackle, however, should only brush his man as he drives to the opponent's inside and hurry to block the safety. The brush-block by the tackle is sufficient in this situation, for the linebacker is picked up by the right guard after he has set his man up for the trap.

The left guard and the center are assigned a cross-charge block to remove the defensive guards from the point of attack. To perform this job effectively, both blockers should step first with their inside foot. The center goes first, but the guard need not delay or pull back off the line if both offensive players will start with their inside foot. Since the defensive guard will likely direct his charge at the pulling guard, the center must remember to lead him far enough to get his head in front of the defender and prevent penetration.

The left guard should remember that, as the trapper on the play, he should direct his block at a point one foot behind the defensive man. This method of trap blocking assures the guard that the defender cannot drop off the line and get back in front of the ball.

The first responsibility of the right guard is to influence the defensive guard to stay on the line of scrimmage, so that the latter may be trapped by the offensive left guard. He may best carry out this assignment by firing out, hitting the outside shoulder of his opponent. This action will give the defender the impression that the blocker is trying to take him to his inside. His natural resistance, therefore, will hold him on the line and cause him to try to get wider. The right guard releases quickly to pick up the linebacker after the tackle has brushed by him.

The quarterback steps up to receive the ball from the center, then executes a reverse pivot on his right foot. At this point the quarterback should give the ball to the left halfback in the regular manner. After the hand-off, the quarterback should continue his roll-out and should fake pitching a lateral to the fullback. He finishes his assignment by faking around the end just as he does on the Quick Pitch.

The fullback and right halfback fake wide around toward the sideline and up the field with the identical maneuver they use on the Quick Pitch.

The left halfback should start for the spot on the ground where the ball was held by the center before the snap. Running at top speed, the halfback should take the ball from the quarterback and break through the line just off the left hip of the trapping guard. By hitting quickly the halfback should gain some yardage, even though a good block does not result from the trap.

The Flanker Plays. The last phase of these special plays is a particular play for a particular secondary adjustment. Often an opponent will adopt a definite pattern for meeting flanker sets and give the offense an opportunity to strike the weakness successfully.

One of the most common adjustments by the defense when a left halfback is crossed to the right flat, is to move the corner linebacker up on the line of scrimmage in front of the linebacker. The remainder of the back-field is balanced into a normal three-deep secondary by dropping the corner linebacker on the opposite side back to a halfback position. (Note Figure 74.)

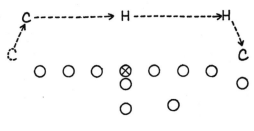

Fig. 74.

To insure that the offense will not be stuck with an unsuccessful play should the defensive secondary fail to revolve toward the flanker, this play should be an automatic. The team comes out of the huddle with the Flanker Reverse called, but if the defense has failed to shift toward the flanker, the quarterback should give the automatic call to run the Flanker Pitch toward the flanker.

The Flanker Reverse. The Flanker Reverse is particularly effective against the *Professional* or *Eagles' Defense* that revolves its secondary to meet the crossed flanker.

The left end and left tackle block in on the defenders aligned to their inside.

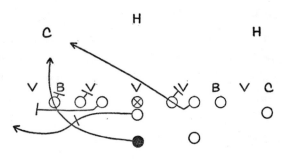

Fig. 75.

The left guard pulls to block the defensive end and tries to move him out and back. The guard should stay near the line of scrimmage and approach the end from a point behind the defender to make his block easier.

The center and right guard block the man in front in the normal manner. At the same time, the right tackle pulls around the guard to gain a step as he goes downfield and tries to reach the defensive halfback before the ball. This method is most effective in releasing from the line of scrimmage. A shallow path is necessary for the tackle to reach the secondary defender in time.

The right end and the flanked left halfback block the defenders in front and aid in carrying out the fake of a play toward the flanker.

The quarterback and the fullback handle the ball just as they do on the Slant Play. After the fullback receives the ball and breaks through the hole, he should make an effort to cut back toward the middle of the field in order to give the right tackle a chance to get his block on the defensive halfback. The quarterback should fake around the end after the hand-off.

The right halfback runs the same course that he takes on the Slant Play and should carry his fake through.

If the defensive end becomes aggressive in forcing the play to the inside over the left guard, the quarterback may keep the ball by running it around the end after a fake to the fullback. With the right halfback leading, this is a strong running play to the outside.

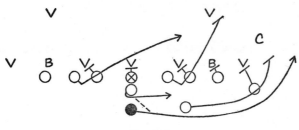

Fig. 76.

The Flanker Pitch. If the defense fails to rotate to meet the flanker, the quarterback may change the Flanker Reverse to the Flanker Pitch. This change may be made from the line of scrimmage by using an automatic call.

The assignments of the Flanker Pitch are identical to that of the Quick Pitch, except that the left halfback is flankered to the right where he blocks back in on the defensive end.

Recognizing and Hitting Your Opponent's Defensive Weaknesses

Unless the attack is carefully planned, it is unrealistic to assume that the offense is going to move the ball well. Each defense aligns its players so that they have more strength at some points than at others. Should we direct our attack toward the opponent's strong points, we could expect little success unless we were superior in manpower. Against strong opposition we must plan carefully to give our players an advantage by directing our attack at the weakness of the defense.

To strike at the weakness of the defense, the offensive team (and especially the quarterback) must be able to identify the defense. The high school coach must teach his players enough about defensive football so that they will be able to recognize the defense. The method for identifying the defense must be simple enough so the players can recognize the alignment quickly under game conditions.

Once the players learn to recognize the defense, they must then learn the weakness of the defense. Merely to be able to recognize the defensive alignment quickly will serve little purpose unless the players can locate the weak points. Knowing the weakness of the defense must be followed by learning the plays that hit that weakness. From the list of plays at his disposal, the quarterback picks the play that strikes at the defensive weakness.

With this, the strategy of the Split-T attack is complete:

(1) Recognize the defense.

(2) Know the weakness of the defense.

(3) Call the plays that hit the weakness.

Recognizing the Defense

I think the easiest method of identifying the defense is to follow three simple steps. First, determine whether the alignment is odd or even. Next, find out if it is a box or three-deep secondary. And third, to complete the job, count the linebackers.

To determine if the defense is even or odd we look to see if there are men playing in front of the offensive guards. If there are no defensive men playing in this area, the defense is odd. Obviously, if there are players aligned in front of the guards, the defense is even.

Having determined that the defense is odd or even, we then turn to the task of recognizing the secondary deployment. This may be done quickly by looking for a safety. If there is a defensive man playing in this position, it is three-deep. With no safety, it is a box secondary.

All that remains is to count the linebackers. Now we have completed our identification. With a little practice the average player can move through these three simple steps very quickly.

To illustrate, let us look at two or three imaginary defensive alignments. On our first defense we find that there are no men playing in front of the guard, so our defense will be an odd alignment. Next we look and see that the opponents have a safety, so we now know they are using an odd defense with three-deep. By counting the linebackers and finding that we have three, we know our defense is a 5-3. By a simple procedure of adding the three deep men to the three linebackers and subtracting the total from eleven, we get the number of linemen.

Our next defense has defenders in front of the guards to make the alignment even. It has a safety for three-deep and there are two linebackers so we know we are facing a 6-2.

Our third imaginary defense has men ahead of the guards but no safety. We count three linebackers and it cannot be anything but a 6-3.

With this method we may quickly recognize all of the common defenses. In order to locate the weakness of all the common defenses, we use our method of identifying them to make a list of all the orthodox alignments. Our first group will include those even defenses deploying the secondary in three deep. Rarely will any team use a two-man line or a ten-man line, so we will only list the fours, sixes, and eights.

Let us consider the common six-man line defenses. The first is a *wide-tackle six,* then the *tight-tackle six* and the *gap six.*

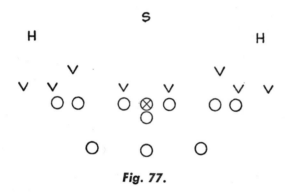

Fig. 77.

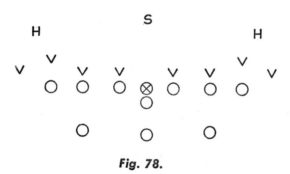

Fig. 78.

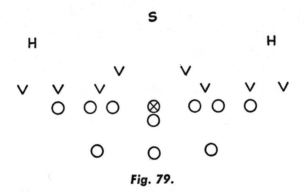

Fig. 79.

There are two more even defenses with three deep. These are the *4-4* and the *eight-man-line*.

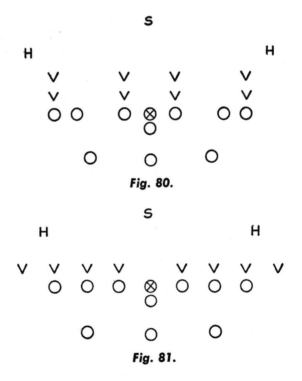

Fig. 80.

Fig. 81.

The even defenses that have a box secondary are these: the *6-3*, the *4-5*, and the *8-1*.

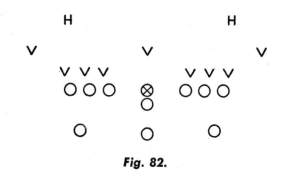

Fig. 82.

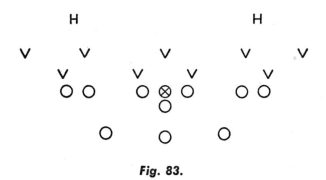

Fig. 83.

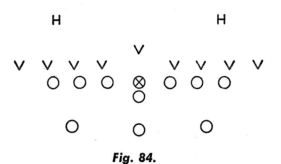

Fig. 84.

Since we seldom see a three-man line—and with the exception of the goal line defenses—nine-man lines are not used to any extent. This leaves only the *7-1* and the *5-3* among the odd defenses with three-deep.

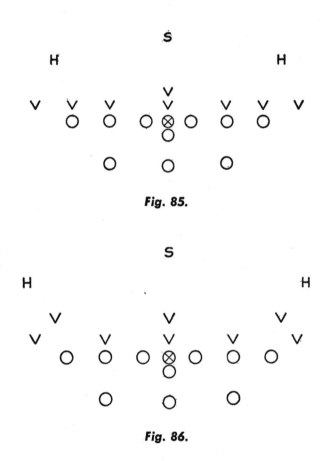

Fig. 85.

Fig. 86.

The last group of defenses is the odd defenses with a box secondary. In this group are the *7-2* and the *5-4*.

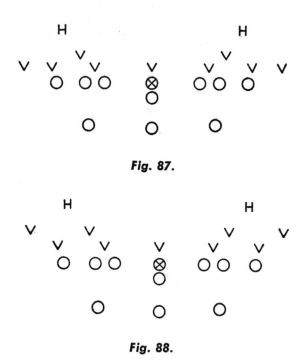

Fig. 87.

Fig. 88.

There are numerous variations to these common defenses but all unusual alignments are related to one of these formations. The similarity of the variations to the basic pattern is so distinct that they usually retain the weakness of the original alignment.

Knowing the Weakness of the Defense

When the offensive players have learned to recognize the defense, their next move is to learn the weakness of each alignment. The weak point of the defensive formation must be located quickly if it is to be exploited. Most high school coaches have learned long ago that they can't expect the average quarterback to survey the entire playing field and pinpoint the defensive weakness. This is too much for the high school player to accomplish in such a short time. For this reason, I think the best method is to consider only a small area at one time.

All offensive plays are directed to the inside, to the outside, or they are passes. For our inside area, we will consider the area inside of the offensive tackles. By concentrating on this middle area, it will not be so difficult to find a possible weakness.

The next area that we will consider in search of a weakness is the territory outside of the tackles. These small areas are usually defended with no more than two or three players, so they can be analyzed immediately.

The third area is the secondary, where the offense can size up the situation quickly, for all secondaries are deployed in box or three-deep.

As we consider each of the common defenses, we will start with the middle area and seek a weakness inside the tackles. We will look at the defensive alignment outside the tackles next as an indication of the strength against a wide run. Our last survey will be made in the secondary. The first group of defenses was the even-three-deep alignments and from this group we will choose the wide-tackle-six for our consideration.

As we check the wide-tackle-six, we notice that in the middle area the opponents have two players stationed inside the offensive tackles. The offense has three blockers—the guards and the center—to handle the two defenders. With the ratio of three-to-two, it is apparent

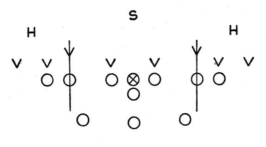

Fig. 89.

that if the attack is directed to this point it will have
a good chance of succeeding.

Now let us look at our second area on the wide-tackle-
six. By checking Figure 89, we see that the defensive
team has three players facing our two offensive blockers
—the tackle and end. This area is not as inviting as the
middle area, for here the ratio of defensive men to
blockers is reversed. Since we are outnumbered in the
outside area, it would not be advisable to try to move
the ball there.

In the third area, the secondary, we know that all defenses are deployed in one of two alignments, *box or
three-deep,* so when we see the wide-tackle-six is using
a safety man, we recognize that we are dealing with a
three-deep secondary.

As we evaluate the three-deep secondary, it is apparent that a pass down the middle of the field would have
little chance of success, because the safety man is stationed there. Since the defensive halfbacks do not have
to protect this middle area on passes, they can rotate up
quickly and reinforce the outside linemen. Evaluating

this possibility, we realize that unless we can keep the defensive halfback away from the line of scrimmage, the defense will be too strong to run in this area. By forcing the halfback to play deep against the possibility of a pass, we can give the offense a better chance to operate. For this reason the run-pass option plays become more attractive in this situation. The defensive halfback is eliminated, for he cannot come up quickly with a receiver coming into his territory. The quarterback may create a weakness in the three-deep secondary by basing his attack on the run-pass options.

From our second group of defenses, the odd-three deep, we will pick the 5-3 to check the three areas for weaknesses.

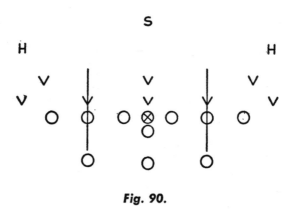

Fig. 90.

Notice in examining the middle area of the 5-3 that the opponents have only two men inside our tackles. One of these defensive players is a linebacker, so the alignment has only one defender on the line of scrimmage. This makes the middle area so attractive that we feel the quarterback should base his attack on plays that strike here.

The outside area of the 5-3 does not appear to be so attractive, since three defensive men are aligned here. However, we have learned that the normal defensive pattern calls for the ends to crash on the 5-3 defense. A crashing end moves so aggressively toward the quarterback on the Option Play that he is not able to recover after the lateral. For this reason the crashing end of the 5-3 defense may be handled easily by the quarterback, making the wide area weak.

The secondary of the 5-3 is three-deep, so the Option Pass that would keep the defensive halfback from supporting the linemen would hit a weakness in the secondary and still take advantage of the crashing ends.

Our next group of defenses is the even-Box alignments. In this group we will analyze the 6-3 by checking the three areas for a weakness.

A glance at the middle area of the 6-3 shows that this area is not inviting. There are now three defenders in-

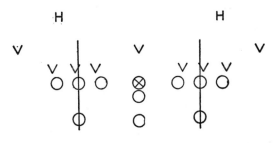

Fig. 91.

side our tackles and unless we are superior in manpower we will not be able to move the ball well with man-for-man blocking. It will be more profitable to try to direct the offensive attack to the other areas.

The area outside the tackles is defended by three men on the 6-3, but one of these defenders is the corner linebacker. This corner linebacker is a member of the secondary and is charged with pass defense responsibilities. For this reason the outside area is not as strongly defended as would appear at first glance. By sending receivers into the corner defender's area, our quarterback may eliminate his support along the line and our blockers will have to deal with only the defensive linemen.

The secondary of the 6-3 is defended with a box alignment that is vulnerable to deep passes down the middle since there is no safety man. To compensate for this weakness, the defensive halfbacks are moved closer together than they are on the three-deep. These defensive halfbacks are coached to prevent, at any cost, the long, easy touchdown pass down the middle. They will be held in an inside deep position by a threat of a pass. Any play that threatens the middle with a pass will cause the halfback to drop back to the inside and deep, creating a wide area for the corner linebacker to protect. This maneuver gives us a weakness to exploit.

We have one more group of common defenses, the Odd Box, and from this group we will investigate the 5-4.

The middle area of the 5-4 is protected by three men, but the splitting of the offensive guards has isolated the

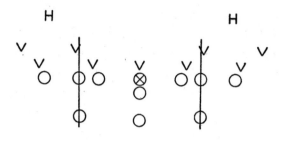

Fig. 92.

middle guard. For this reason we may base our attack in the middle area.

The outside area and the secondary are aligned exactly as they were on the 6-3. In fact, we find that there will be very little variation in these areas on any of the defenses using a box secondary. We can expect, therefore, to encounter the same weaknesses.

Hitting the Weakness

After having recognized the defense and learned the weakness of the alignment, the quarterback's most important assignment is to call the plays that hit the weakness.

Once the defensive weakness is located, the offense must exercise a great deal of tenacity by hitting this weakness again and again. The most effective method of putting the pressure on the defense is to find the plays that hit the weakness of the alignment and stick with them until the defense changes.

I know of no easy way for the quarterback to learn the plays that strike at the weakness of the defense. The high school coach should go over each of the common alignments with his quarterback and suggest two or three plays for this purpose. The player should then draw a chart showing the defense and the plays that have been assigned to each one. His task of memorizing these plays will be easier if no more than three plays are given. Three plays will be enough to move the ball well if they are chosen carefully.

With this ability, the Split-T quarterback can carry out his complete duty as a field general. He must be able to recognize the defense quickly, locate the weakness, and call only those plays that hit that weakness.

As we consider the phase of the quarterback's duties of calling the plays that hit the weakness, let us look again at the defensive alignments we studied to locate the weakness. Our first defense was the wide-tackle six from the even three-deep series. We decided that the wide-tackle six was weak in the middle area. To hit this area we choose three plays, the Hand-off, the Counter, and from among the specials, the Quick Trap. Naturally, we would not recommend that all three plays assigned to the quarterback for the wide-tackle defense, strike at the middle area, so we would take only one or two for each game. The first is the Hand-off.

To exploit the weakness in the middle area, we have started with the Hand-off. We may expect to move the ball effectively as long as the defenders play in an orthodox manner. A stunt by the linebacker would not hamper the play, since the halfback may cut to the outside behind the tackle's block in case the linebacker shoots to

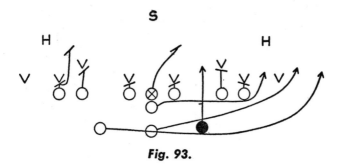

Fig. 93.

the inside. However, if the defensive guard playing ahead of the right offensive guard should slide out, he might stop the play. To meet this possibility the quarterback could change to the Counter Play and force the sliding guard to move just as we would like him to go.

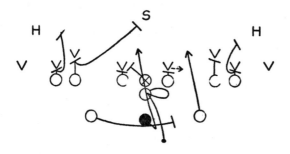

Fig. 94.

By using the Hand-off and Counter together we are able to put considerable pressure on the middle area of the defense, but our third play also strikes quickly at this weak point. The Quick Trap that employs a crossblock by the guards and the center to open a hole in the defensive middle will cause our opponents more trouble.

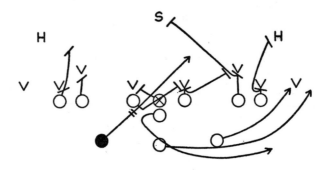

Fig. 95.

As we look at the area outside the tackles on the wide-tackle six, we remember that we decided that this territory was well defended. We will not find a weakness here unless we carry out the run-pass option that will keep the defensive halfback from moving up quickly. For this reason we choose the Option Pass.

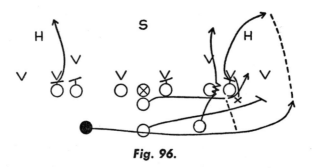

Fig. 96.

From the second group, the odd three-deep defenses, we chose the 5-3 to investigate for weaknesses. We decided the middle area was one of the best potential points of attack, so we will instruct our quarterback to rely on the Hand-off and Counter. The Hand-off permits the halfback to cut to the open side of the tackle's block, while the guard and end pick off the linebackers to prevent them from filling in.

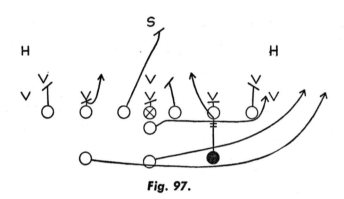

Fig. 97.

One adjustment can be made that will help a great deal in running the Counter Play against the 5-3. Since the defensive guard in front of the left tackle has a tendency to slide to the inside with a flow of play, it is better for the left guard to block out on this defender, cutting off his pursuit. The tackle may pull around behind the guard to reach the linebacker.

The middle linebacker should move toward the fake of the halfback and be in a poor position to defend himself against the tackle's block. The counter step of the fullback will delay his forward movement so that he will arrive at the line of scrimmage just behind the tackle.

In checking the outside area of the 5-3, we found it was weak because of the crashing ends. Since the outside linebacker has to move from behind the line of

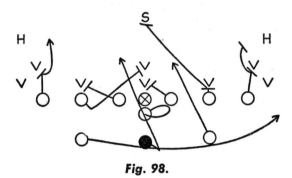

Fig. 98.

scrimmage to meet the outside attack, he is poorly positioned to meet the fullback's block on the Option Play. For these reasons, we feature the Option Play against the outside weakness of the 5-3.

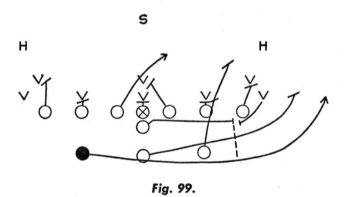

Fig. 99.

If the defense meets the pressure of the Option Play by rotating quickly to allow the defensive halfback to come up and force the play, we should change to the Option Pass. The pass threat will keep the halfback from coming up and the change will not hurt the blocking of the offensive team, since the ends are free—that is, there are no defenders on the line of scrimmage in front of them.

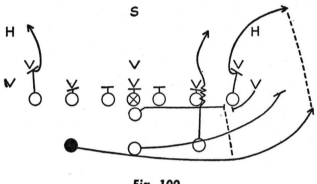

Fig. 100.

Our examination of the 6-3 as one of the group of Even Box defenses revealed that the middle area was not a weak point. The outside area promises more chance of success, especially if we threaten a pass to freeze the defensive halfback in position. We will then instruct our quarterback to try the Quick Pass and the Slant Pass

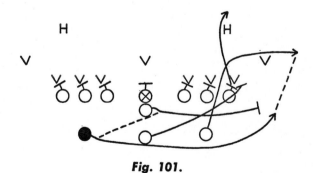

Fig. 101.

for this purpose. Let us look at the Quick Pass first as a means of hitting the weakness of the outside area of the 6-3.

The Slant Pass will put the pressure on the corner linebacker if the defensive end is forced to respect the fullback's fake. Our quarterback should be instructed to call the Slant Play when the end ignores the fullback. The Slant makes the defensive end protect to his inside. With this defender out of the way, the corner linebacker is always wrong. If he comes up, he may be blocked by the left halfback and leave the right halfback open for an easy pass. If the corner man stays back, the quarterback will run with the ball with the left halfback leading.

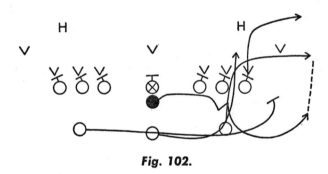

Fig. 102.

If our opponents should rotate quickly with the flow of the play, they might hamper the Quick Pass and the Slant Pass. However, we should be ready for this eventuality by realizing that their rotation has exposed a weakness that we may hit with the Shield Reverse.

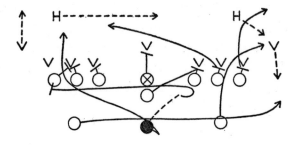

Fig. 103.

The Box Secondary deploys nine players, linemen and linebackers, within 3 yards of the line of scrimmage. With only the two halfbacks as deep pass defenders, our offense has an excellent *gamble play* in the Counter Pass. If successful, the Counter Pass will likely be a very long gainer and has a good chance of going all the way to a touchdown. The defense is so frightened by this possibility that even when the pass is incomplete, the linebackers will move off the line where they are not so tough against our running attack.

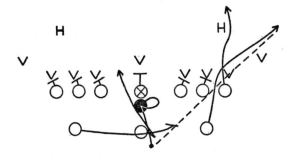

Fig. 104.

We picked a 5-4 defense to represent our last group, the Odd Box defenses. Our examination revealed a weakness in the middle area that may be attacked with the Hand-off and Counter. Proper splitting is a prerequisite to the success of these plays, since the middle guard must be isolated.

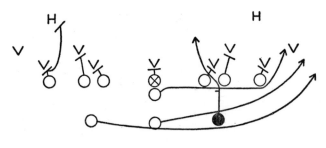

Fig. 105.

If the middle guard slides to meet the threat of the Hand-off, we may use this move in the wrong direction to hit the defense with the Counter Play.

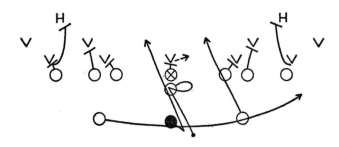

Fig. 106.

Our particular 5-4 defense presents a new problem to our attack in the outside area. In this alignment, the

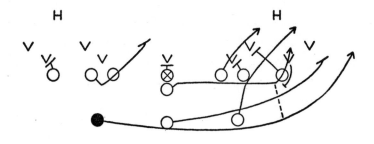

Fig. 107.

inside linebackers are stationed on the outside shoulders of the offensive tackles and may help defend the outside against the Quick Pass and the Slant Pass. For this reason we would give preference to the Option Play against this 5-4, for the offensive end can cut off the pursuit to the outside by the linebacker. The right halfback has no blocking assignment in the line and can lead the blocking downfield. We would base our attack on the Option Play on this 5-4.

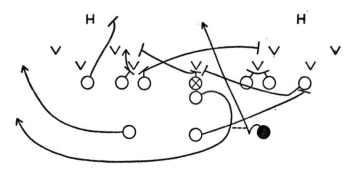

Fig. 108.

These wide inside linebackers on this 5-4 defense give us an excellent opportunity to hit the weakness with one of our specials, the End Trap.

Since some opponents will change the defensive alignment almost every down, they may catch us in a bad situation in which the defense is no longer deployed in the formation for which the play has been called. To be certain that we can hit the weakness, we must be able to change the play from the line of scrimmage. To avoid running an unsuccessful play, the ability to check the play from the line of scrimmage is essential to the successful operation of the Split-T. The Split-T attack with its limited number of basic plays makes the maneuver much easier than it might be with other offensive formations.

The easiest method is to give each of the basic running plays a single digit number. The number indicates the point of attack for each of the basic plays. It will not be necessary to designate the ball-carrier after you have identified the play, for high school players will always know who is to carry the ball. A numbering system for the running plays is suggested in Figure 109 that will lend itself to checking readily.

With this system, if the quarterback wants to change the hand-off on the right side (number two) to the Option Play on the same side (number six) he says "Check, add 4." If he has called the Slant Play on the left (number five) and sees a weakness that the Counter on the left (number one) would hit, he calls, "Check, drop 4." With the arithmetic being so simple, the average player can perform it in a very short time.

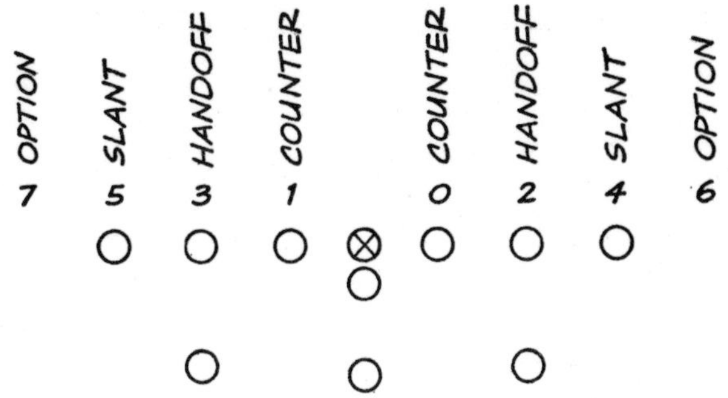

Fig. 109.

It is also very simple to change the pass plays on the line of scrimmage. We can change from a running play to a pass play or from a pass play to a running play just as easily. The pass plays are given the numerals from 10 through 19, but in checking the play at the line of scrimmage we only consider the second digit of the number. Since all of the pass plays develop off a running play fake, we have the pass plays use the same second digit as the running play to which it is similar.

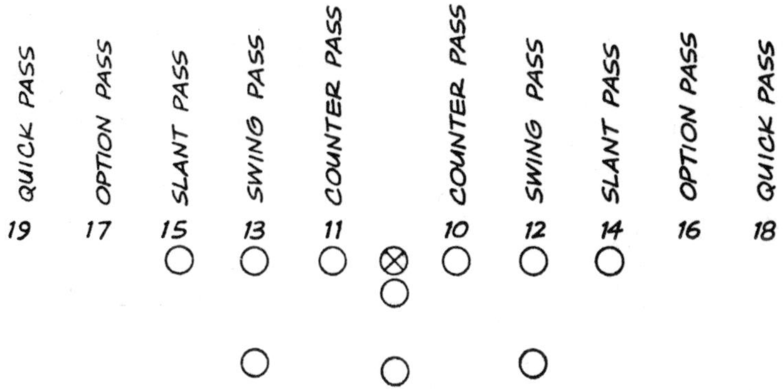

Fig. 110.

If we are going to change a running play to a pass play, we use the word "change" instead of "check." Of course, we change from a pass play to a running play by the same signal, but if we had a pass play called and would like to change it to another pass play, we would use the word "check."

Let us take a few examples of changes we might make on the line of scrimmage. Suppose the Slant Pass (number fourteen) is called in the huddle. After arriving at the line of scrimmage, however, the quarterback decides the Quick Pass on the left (number nineteen) would do better. He calls, "Check, add 5." However, should the quarterback want to change to a running play after he had called the Slant Pass in the huddle, he might call, "Change, drop 1," to run the Hand-off on the left. In this case the team would remember to consider the second digit of the double number and subtract one from four to get three, the hand-off number.

With this ability to change the play on the line of scrimmage, the team should never run a bad play. The quarterback may ably direct the Split-T attack if he can *recognize the defense, learn the weakness of the defense* and always *call the plays that hit the weakness.*

9 Developing Your Offensive Game Strategy

It is an accepted fact that success in coaching depends not so much on a coach's knowledge of football as on his ability to teach. Most coaches have discovered that when they have tried to use plays in a game that were not taught well, they got into trouble. Remember that there are an unlimited number of excellent plays, drills, and formations, all of which would be worthwhile if the coach had the time to teach them to his players. It therefore seems advisable that a coach have an offensive game plan that will limit his attack to plays he has had time to teach thoroughly.

In high school football, organization and careful planning are more important than brilliant strategy. I have known a few men who were very intelligent but were never successful in the coaching field. These coaches could prove their offensive strategy on the blackboard by beating any defense in theory, but failed to get this information across to their players. Although the coach may have a wealth of information, it will be of little value unless it is made available to the players before the game. The best method of presenting this vital information and eliminating all of the unessentials is to use a definite offensive game plan.

This plan should be made by the coach and presented to the team early in the week before the game, in order that they may have plenty of time to learn the offensive strategy. In it the coach will evaluate and summarize all the information available—using such sources as the scout report and the movies of previous games—and present them in a brief, concise report. This report points out any patterns of play, tendencies to do the same thing every time a certain situation arises, or other habits the defensive team may have formed that will reveal their defensive strategy.

The coach will not only give his players the characteristics of the defense that will help detect its weaknesses, but he will suggest the plays that exploit these weaknesses most effectively. It is unrealistic to expect the average high school player to make these specific adjustments during the height of the game. However, if the quarterback knows what he is looking for, and knows definitely what plays he will call when he finds it, he should be able to direct the offensive team efficiently.

The Scout Report

In mapping the details of his offensive game plan, the coach can gather important information from the scout report. One of the first things to look for is a favorite defense. Most teams have a favorite defensive alignment upon which they will rely when they get into difficulty. Although these defensive teams may start the game with different alignments, they will fall back on their old pattern if the offense begins to move the ball effectively. Since they use their favorite defense often, they will show more confidence when using it and will execute their familiar assignments quite well. Unless the offense is ready with special preparation and the quarterback knows exactly what plays he is to call, the favorite defense of the opponents will make it rough for the attack to move the ball. New alignments may surprise the attacking team, but if they were installed after only two or three days of practice and have never been tried in a game, they are not usually effective as the game goes along. However, if the opponent catches the offense unprepared for the basic alignment they have been using the entire season, they will give them a difficult time. The game plan can help the team prepare for the opponent's defense that is going to give them the most trouble.

The scout report may point out certain defensive tendencies. Some defensive teams establish a pattern in dealing with certain game situations. They may jump into a tight, goal-line type of defense on each short yardage situation, trying to force a fumble by the offensive team. If this pattern is picked up by the scout and emphasized in the game plan, the quarterback may operate more smoothly. The signal caller can anticipate a tight defense on short yardage and call a wide play.

This method will save time and confuse the defense more than checking to a wide play on the line of scrimmage.

Another defensive pattern practiced by some teams is to use a special defense, usually a loose 5–3, on long yardage. They believe this type of defense will help them defend better against a pass. Against a team that is following this pattern, the coach should suggest in the plan that a hand-off or trap be used in preference to a pass on long yardage situations. The basic rule of strategy for the Split-T is: *Anticipate what the defense is expecting, then do the opposite.* A game plan will keep the quarterback from violating this rule.

The scout report may show the opponents to be wide-field conscious—that is, they deploy their strength toward the open field. In this case, the coach should suggest in his plan that the majority of the plays be run from the hash-marks into the sideline.

Other tendencies that might be revealed in the scout report and are a useful part of the game plan are: The opponents may change defenses from down to down. This means it is imperative that the quarterback be alert in recognizing the defense and check to the right play every time. The opponents may like to try to confuse the offense by jumping from one defense to another after the team has lined up on the line of scrimmage. To meet this maneuver, the quarterback should call every play on a quick count. If the pass defense is not as strong as the running defense, the offense should be instructed to throw more passes. If the scout report shows the opponents to have a very strong offensive team, the game plan should stress the importance of maintaining possession. If we can hold on to the ball, we cut down the time we will have to play defense.

Special Game Instructions

There is additional information that should be included in the game plan, since it is to our advantage to change our procedure often, thus avoiding tendencies that show up in the game that might help the defense. The first of this group is that the coach should instruct the team on how he expects them to handle the kicking game. It is a very good rule to punt on third down inside your 35-yard line, but if you form a habit of doing this every time the situation occurs, the defense is going to take advantage of your pattern of play. Some teams use a quick kick after every penalty inside their thirty-yard line. Although this is also a fine rule, if we do it every time, we are certain to get a kick blocked sooner or later. The coach can break any pattern or habit by instructing his team to handle the kicking differently each game.

Since the quarterback should know definitely what he will call if he starts his offense inside his own 10-yard line, this situation should be covered in the game plan. A fumble, or losing the ball, in this area, means an almost automatic touchdown for the opponents. We want our offense to keep the ball handling at a minimum here.

However, we should not try to get out of this hole with the same plays every time, so a different list of conservative plays should be suggested for each opponent.

Certainly no coach wants his signal caller guessing what he will do on the other end of the field while trying to drive the ball in from the opponent's 10-yard line to score. In this area the defense is usually very aggressive in trying to penetrate the gaps between our linemen, so we like to use only quick, straight-ahead plays. However, if we use the same ones every time, we might forfeit our opportunity to score. We can get away from any such tendencies to repeat by selecting for each game the plays we will use to score.

Our plan should tell our team what plays we will use to conserve time if we are behind in the score near the end of the half or late in the game. It should also tell our quarterback what he would call if we are ahead, and he wants to use up the time remaining near the end of these two periods.

The Offensive Game Plan

The plan will have five sections. The first section—the introduction—will contain a few statements that relate specifically to this particular game: this contest's importance to our standing in the conference; the rating a victory would give us among the state's top teams and the intense rivalry between the two schools; the opponent's characteristics that will affect the offense to be used; and encouraging comments that should give our team confidence that we will win with our best effort.

The second portion of the play will list the defenses that this opponent has used in previous games. A diagram should be made by the coach illustrating how the linemen should split, and suggesting at least three plays for each alignment.

The next section merely lists our offense. This is a reliable method of preventing the number of plays from growing so large that it overtaxes the players to remember their assignments. The quarterback should be instructed never to use any unlisted play, unless by special permission by the coach.

The fourth section tells how we will use any flankers or special plays in this game.

The last entry in the plan will be a summary, emphasizing in about ten statements those most important points that we should like the team to remember.

Hypothetical Game Plan

Central has never defeated us on our home field and they are most determined to do so Friday night. A victory over the Bulldogs will give us the District 6A Championship.

Central is a big, inspired team. At the start of the game they will charge harder in the line than any team we have played. The Bulldogs will continue to play hard until we show them that we are just as determined as they are. We can have things our way in the last half if we keep the pressure on the defense the entire game. Our best chance to win will be to wear them down physically.

Their defense has been stronger inside than outside. As a result, we should plan on basing our offense on wide plays at the start of the game. The Option Play, the Quick Pass, and the Option Pass should be good against any defense they will use. Since the middle portion of their defense pursues very rapidly, reverses should be excellent. Use the Shield Reverse to the narrow side of the field. Run the Quick Cutback several times at the start of the game.

They have shown a definite weakness against play passes. We should use the Counter Pass and the Slant Pass often. Use these plays when you would normally throw a pass. You should figure the Quick Pass and the Option Pass as running plays this week and not as passes.

You must be ready to check to the right plays for each of their defenses. Central was rather effective against us last season by using a tight, cross-charging defense. When they are in a typical cross-charge situation, that is, with a linebacker directly behind the end, you must check to the Quick Pitch. If, however, they jump their linebackers up into the line in the gaps between their linemen, you must check to the Option Play or the

Option Pass. Study this. Make the check mentally. Be sure that you can handle this.

We have two special plays this week. The first time we get the ball, use one of these plays and if it is good, use the other. If both plays are successful, use them until the Bulldogs make some adjustment to them. Call these plays according to lateral field position:

1. If the ball is on our left hash-mark, use Spread Pitch.
2. If the ball is on our right hash-mark, use Spread Left Pitch.
3. In the middle of the field you may call either.

We will win or lose the game on effort. Force them to run out of stamina as the game goes along. If we play fast enough, we can win in the fourth quarter. Remember, this game is for the District Championship.

Central's Defenses

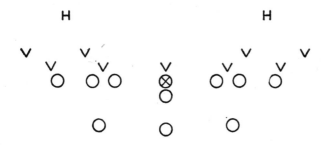

Fig. 111. Regular 5-4 Defense. Plays to use: Hand-off; Counter; Option Play.

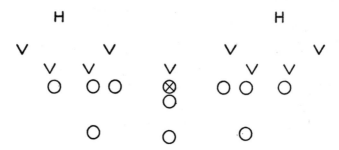

Fig. 112. Inside 5-4. Plays to use: *Hand-off; Counter; Quick Pass.*

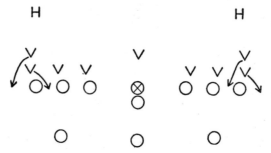

Fig. 113. 6-3 Cross-Charge. Plays to use: *Quick Pitch.* (Be certain you are alert when they use this cross-charge and check to the play indicated.)

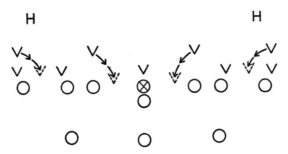

Fig. 114. Gaps. Plays to use: *Option Play; Option Pass.* (Be sure you recognize this defensive maneuver and check to the plays suggested.)

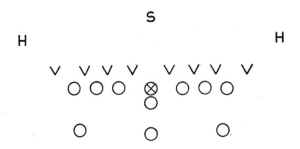

Fig. 115. Goal-Line Defense. Plays to use: *Option Play; Option Pass; Slant Pass.*

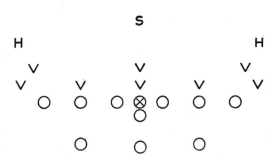

Fig. 116. 5-3 Defense. Plays to use: *Hand-Off; Counter; Option Pass. (Use only the plays indicated against this alignment. Do not throw a pass against this alignment.)*

Offense vs. Central

Basic Plays	*Basic Passes*	*Reverses*	*Flankers*
Hand-off	Counter Pass	Swing Pass	1. Slant Pass
Counter	Slant Pass	Quick Reverse	2. Swing Pass
Slant	Option Pass	Shield Reverse	
Option	Quick Pass		

Specials	*Particular Plays for Particular Defenses*
Spread Right Pitch	Quick Trap
Spread Left Pitch	Quick Pitch

Use of Flankers

Fig. 117. Slant Pass. Swing Pass. (Use these flankers near the end of the half or late in the game if you are behind.)

Summary

1. Do not become discouraged with our offense if we do not move the ball well in the first half. We will understand the defense by the start of the second half and should be able to play well on offense during the last 24 minutes.

2. Quick kick on second or third down if we have more than 7 yards to go for a first down and are behind the 50-yard line.

3. Punt on second down inside our twenty if we have more than 5 yards to go for a first down during the first half of the game.

4. Repeat the plays that are successful. Do not surrender the ball without repeating a play that has helped us to make a first down.

5. Be ready to check signals every down, but try not to delay our attack by doing so. Check only when it is necessary.

6. On the goal line, use the Hand-off to the right and the Option to the left. If our line is not out-charging the opponents, use the Quick Pass and the Slant Pass on the third and fourth down. However, if our linemen are moving the defensive players, run the Hand-off on the left and the Option on the right.

7. Do not transfer the ball inside our 10-yard line. Call the Option Play to each side, but don't lateral. Run with the ball yourself. Punt on the third down if you do not get the ball out in two plays.

8. We should plan on basing our attack on wide runs and the run-pass option. These plays together with reverses to the narrow side of the field should be our best offense.

9. You must use our passing attack against Central. Be sure you pass enough to keep them loosened up but try to keep incompleted passes from keeping us from making first down.

10. As always, our offense will succeed or fail on your ability to speed up the tempo of our play to the point that the defense cannot stand the pace. Use a balanced attack and be physically tougher than Central.

Chapter

10

Using Mechanical and
Visual Coaching Aids

Some of the devices that are being manufactured to aid the coach with his teaching are most interesting. The coach with sufficient financial resources may have blocking sleds ranging from a one-man sled to a seven-man sled. He may purchase various mechanical tackling dummies, some of which are powered by a motor. There are blocking chutes that assure that the blocker will charge out in a low, straight line, since his path is lined with metal pipes. The backfield is not neglected since there are bucking harnesses that teach the backfield man to hold his feet while driving out against the resistance of an elastic rope held by his teammates. A rope maze has replaced the old automobile tires in teaching the ball-carrier the high knee action that all coaches desire.

Blocking dummies are now constructed in all sizes and shapes. The inflated type may be carried by the defensive players as they move about in carrying out their assignments. The most common type—the old upright bag—may now be filled with light foam rubber that is so light the dummy can be carried easily by one player. A blocking armor inflated with air may be used to suit up the defensive players to protect them from injury when they are blocked.

Due to lack of time and practice space on the field, we use only a few mechanical aids, although many of them are helpful in high school coaching. As we have explained earlier, we use the two-man blocking sled because with only one or two men performing, we are able to watch more critically than we could if more players were in action at one time. We use the old style, upright blocking dummy, which is 52 inches tall and weighs about 90 pounds. This heavier dummy gives about the right amount of resistance while the blockers are driving them off the boards. The boards are two by twelves, 10 feet in length, and are used to teach the blockers to keep their feet apart and to drive straight-ahead while blocking. The backfield men also use a board—a one by six that is 3 feet in length—to run over while learning to go straight into the exchange point while taking a hand-off. These are all the mechanical aids we use on the practice field.

The Duplicating Machine

The duplicating machine is one of several devices that we use in connection with classroom lectures. In fact, the direct process duplicating machine is almost indispensable, for it enables us to produce 40 or 50 copies of timely information and present them to the players for individual study in a matter of minutes. The operation of this type of duplicator is so simple that no special skill is required. Stencils may be typed and run through the machine quickly by a member of the coaching staff. Since the copies may be turned out so rapidly, the coaches may delay their reports until they have had time to discuss the material thoroughly and decide definitely what information should be included.

We start our preparation for a game by running the copies of our defense against the opponent through the machine as early in the week as possible. Since most high school games in our area are played on Friday, we expect our scout to turn in his report by Sunday. The coaching staff immediately checks the offense of the opponents and decides on a defense. The assignments for each defensive position are typed out on a stencil and the copies are run off so each player may have his copy of the defense on Monday morning.

This method permits the player to refer to his defensive assignment any time during the week and allows the coaching staff to devote more of their practice time to other things. We use a system of assigning the players to their positions by using their jersey numbers. This method of identification takes up a very small space on the reports but tells the player exactly where he will play. With this information, each player may concentrate on his assignment.

To prevent a copy of the defense from being lost and possibly getting into the hands of the opponents, the copies are checked out with the player's name on it and are carefully checked back in on Friday morning. We try to be as strict as possible in the observance of this rule and expect every player to account for his copy of defenses. If the player is impressed with the importance of keeping his defensive assignment close at hand, he will likely consult it more often.

The duplicating machine will also be used to make copies of the offensive game plan. We try to complete our offensive plans by Tuesday. This delay will give the coaching staff more time to decide definitely what will be included in the offensive strategy, and will permit the players to consider their defensive assignments for a day before moving to the offensive plan.

There are other items that might be copied on the duplicating machine and given to the players. The offensive and defensive lineups through the first three teams may be distributed on the day of the game so that everyone will know his assignments. Since we have free substitution in high school, we often assign a special team to cover the kickoff. Special players are sent in to kick extra points, to receive punts, and to perform other special duties. These special assignments should be included in this game-day bulletin. When the team is going out of town on a trip, additional information should be included, such as the time the bus will leave, the time of the pre-game meal, and the approximate time of return.

Moving Pictures

The most important visual aid to coaching is moving

pictures. It is difficult to say just how the movies are most helpful, but certainly there is no better way to point out the player's mistakes. Often a boy is not completely convinced that he is performing his assignment poorly even though he might have been told of his mistakes several times by the coaching staff. Since there is no disagreement when he sees his performance in the moving pictures, each player can check his own awkward performance.

As it is merely human nature for each player to be especially attentive and alert when he sees himself on the screen, he will be quick to spot his own errors.

By using a grading system with the movies, the coach is able to create some competition among the players for a better performance. The method we use for grading the pictures is to have the coach rate each player as he operates the projector, with the individual players being allowed to record their own scores. Each player has a paper divided into three columns. In the first column the players write the number of the play as it is being projected. He records in the second section the score that the coach gives his performance. The last space is reserved for a short comment for each play on which he scores poorly. When action on the play is below average, the coach will point out the reason for his failure. The statements should be short, usually consisting of two or three words such as, "hit too low," or "didn't get off on the count." By checking the score sheet, the player can review the reasons for his failures and will often find that he is making the same mistake over and over.

A projector with a reversal switch that permits the play to be run over and over, is essential for this grading method. The coach reverses the projector until each player is graded on his performance on the play. The evaluations are made by the coach by crediting the player with a score of from zero to four. Only an extraordinary performance rates a four. If the player does just what he is supposed to do, we give him two. If he should fail altogether in his assignment, he is given zero.

Another way the movies will help is by showing the trends and patterns of the opponent's play from the picture of last season's game. This will be especially helpful if the opponents still have the same coach and some of the same key players that they had a year ago. Even current films may be obtained by trading pictures with a school that played the opponent earlier in the season.

Moving pictures, by keying the first movements of the offensive team to determine whether the play is a pass or run, provide one of the best methods of teaching defense. This may be done by stopping the film just after the first movements on a play and asking the defensive players to tell if the play is a pass or run. They can learn to read from the first few steps of the offensive linemen what type of play is being run. For example, if one of the five interior linemen crosses the line of scrimmage, the opponents can't run a legal pass play. So if none of these linemen start downfield to block, it indicates that a pass play is most likely. This same procedure, when applied to the game film when our team is on offense, may be used by the offensive linemen to check their pass protection blocks to see if they are concealing the intent to pass as long as possible.

Many college coaches will loan their films to high school coaches. This provides a method of showing the various plays and techniques being performed by older and more experienced players. To get the most help from college films, the high school coach should carefully preview the picture before showing it to his players. This will enable him to point out successful operations as model plays, and direct the attention of his charges to fundamentals he is trying to teach. A film—high school or college—shown without questions and comments by the coach is of little value.

When his game movies are two years old, the coach should use them as teaching aids by cutting all of the shots of a basic play from the pictures and splicing them into one roll. This film will help inexperienced players learn their operation on the play, since they can see it performed over and over by experienced players under game conditions.

Flash Cards and Film Slides

Large cards, about 12 x 15 inches, may be used in teaching the team to recognize the defense quickly. Since it is important for the offensive team to develop this ability if they are going to split properly and run the right play, the coach should spend some time teaching them to recognize the defense.

Each of the common defenses is drawn out on a card with the diagram large enough to be seen by players in a classroom. The cards are held up for a short period, no longer than 5 seconds, and each player makes the identification by writing the number of the defense. Linemen may be required to indicate how much they would split on each defense and the quarterback may suggest which plays would be most effective. The papers are collected and graded by an assistant coach.

Film slides and a slide projector may make this same teaching method a little more realistic. The slides are made from a picture of 11 men deployed in the defensive alignments. If the photographer will shoot the picture from a step ladder over an offensive line, the defense will have a more game-like appearance. The picture is projected on a screen for 5 seconds and the defense is identified by the squad just as the cards were used.

The Checker Board

One of the best mechanical aids for developing the quarterback is the Checker Board. The quarterback lines up his checkers in an offensive formation while the coach seats himself across the table and lines up his checkers in a defensive alignment. The coach gives the quarterback his problem. He may use a 5-4 defense and tell the quarterback that he has the ball on his own

40-yard line, first down and ten. After the quarterback calls the play, the coach comments on his choice and tells him how much he made on the play. The next situation may be second and eight against a 6-3. The quarterback's reactions to any field position, any down and yardage, score and time to play, may be checked by this device.

The Magnetic Board

To show the splitting of the offensive line and the exact position of the defensive players, a magnetic board is very useful. The board is a sheet of metal 3 x 6 feet, that hangs on the wall.

Small blocks about the size of a dime represent the members of the offensive and defensive teams. These small blocks adhere firmly to the metal sheet because each contains a small magnet. This device will show the lateral spacing of the two alignments clearly.

New Ideas and Problems
With the Split-T

THE FUNDAMENTALS THAT WILL MAKE THE Split-T operate successfully will also produce effective results with other offensive formations. The ability to line up on the ball, get off together on the count and make solid contact with the opponent, will move the ball consistently, regardless of which offensive formation is used. We recognize that the Split-T is no magic formula for reaching success in high school coaching. A nation-wide survey will bear this out, for the championship teams are using a number of different formations. The winning teams are those who block and tackle better, who hit harder than their opponents, and who possess a superior knowledge of football.

The Split-T is one of the most popular formations among the championship teams today because of its simplicity. The greatest asset of the Split-T is the hard-hitting attack, composed of only a few plays, that hit straight-ahead over a broad front. Obviously, a few plays may be taught more thoroughly and more quickly than a great number of plays. The Split-T coach has more time to devote to the fundamentals that make the offense successful. He will be able to teach his players game strategy, for the Split-T has only one basic play for each defensive position. The quarterback is not likely to call an unsuccessful play when he has so few plays from which to choose.

The fast hitting Split-T may strike anywhere along the line with a strong inside fake in the initial movements of each play. The interior defensive linemen must hold firmly against this threat of an inside play so they are unable to pursue the wide play effectively. However, to operate successfully, the Split-T team must be able to run all of the basic offense. The Split-T team that is unable to run the Option Play will lose most of its potential, and would be more successful in some other offense. Trying to run wide by other means breaks the continuity of the remainder of the Split-T plays and renders the attack ineffective.

A number of the offensive problems for some Split-T teams may be solved by working harder and developing the ability to handle the Option Play. I believe that the defense can stop the Hand-off, Counter, and Slant if every play that threatens the inside is actually an inside play and not merely a fake to hold the interior defenders while the play is developing out wide around the end. We teach our team that if we run our complete attack, the defense can never stop us. We may stop ourselves

by making mistakes, but we are going to move the ball
if we avoid mistakes.

New Defensive Patterns

Recently the defense has developed some interesting
ideas in an effort to stop the Split-T. The most successful
of these ideas are the Gap Defenses. The Gap Defenses
are only variations of the six-man line, but they approach the defensive problem of meeting the Split-T
from a different angle. The first of this series was the
Wide Guard Defense.

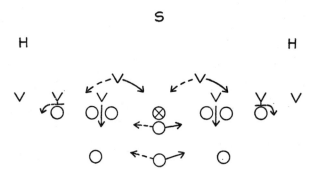

Fig. 118. The Wide Guard Defense.

The Wide Guard Defense caught some Split-T teams
off guard and had considerable success when it was first
introduced. Two hard charging defensive guards were
assigned to play in the gap between the offensive guards
and tackles. By driving hard trying to penetrate this
gap, the defense hoped to tie up the four offensive play-

ers. If either guard or tackle released to block the linebackers, the defensive guards would break into the backfield, so the linebackers were left free to move to the
ball-carrier and make the tackle. The defensive tackles
charged hard into the offensive end, holding him up to
prevent him from blocking the linebackers. They then
moved to the outside, where they joined the defensive
end to protect against a wide play. The linebackers
keyed the movement of the quarterback and the fullback
to cover the hole between the defensive guards and
tackles. This alignment worked well and gave the Split-T
a great deal of trouble until some adjustments were
made to it.

The Split-T coaches soon learned that the Wide
Guard Defense was vulnerable to the hand-off and it is
not as effective as it was when first introduced. The
offense met the challenge of the Wide Guard Defense
by assigning the guard and tackle to double-team the
penetrating guards. The center blocked the linebacker
on the side away from the play and the halfback watched
the linebacker as he took the ball and cut away from
him. (See Figure 119.)

The success of the Wide Guard Defense led the defensive coaches to experiment further with the gap defenses. Another of the most interesting defenses to result from this line of thinking is a Gap 4-5. The Gap 4-5
assigned two defensive men on each side of the line
to the task of trying to penetrate the gaps. The defense
was designed to tie up the entire offensive line while the
linebackers moved unhampered by blocking linemen to

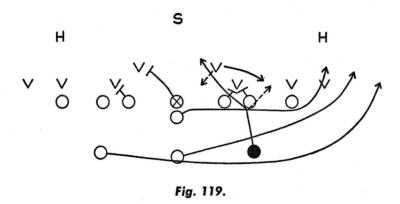

Fig. 119.

stop the play. It is a very flexible defense and can be used against any style of T formation effectively.

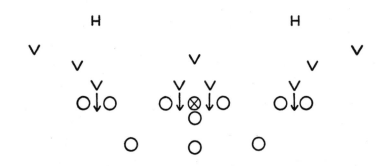

Fig. 120. The Gap 4-5 Defense.

The Split-T is able to cope with the Gap 4-5 Defense by creating a large hole between the penetrating linemen by splitting the offensive tackles. Thus, with no defenders in front of the halfbacks, the Hand-off Play is hard to stop short of the desired 4 yards.

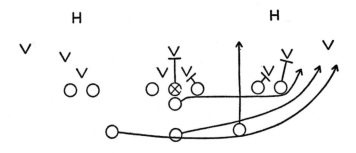

Fig. 121.

If the outside linebacker, who is playing in front of the offensive end, comes to the inside to fill the split, he will leave the outside open for the Option Play.

A currently popular defensive maneuver is to play two defensive men in the gaps between the guards and the center in order to tie up the three offensive players, thereby allowing the middle linebacker to move freely to the point of attack. The theory is that if no offensive lineman can get out of the congested middle fast enough to cut off the linebacker, this defender should stop all plays through the middle of the line. I believe this defensive plan can be handled successfully if the offensive line will split properly and if the quarterback will stick tenaciously to the Hand-off Play to pick up short yardage. Two of the most popular defenses now using the inside gaps and the free linebacker are the Gap Box Defense and the Straight Line Defense. The Gap Box Defense has a box secondary with a standard defensive arrangement in the area outside the tackles.

The most unusual of the gap defenses is a three-deep alignment called the Straight Line Defense. This forma-

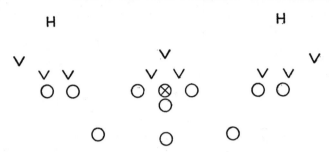

Fig. 122. The Gap Box Defense.

tion receives its name from the fact that it has two line-backers instead of one in front of the offensive center. These two defenders, who are lined up one behind the other, are also in line with the safety, so that the defense has three defensive men in a straight line ahead of the center.

The theory of the Straight Line Defense is that it will be much harder for the offense to fool two linebackers, since one of them is following the quarterback while the other is trailing the fullback. One of the first offensive maneuvers used successfully against the gap defenses was to start the linebacker in the wrong direction by

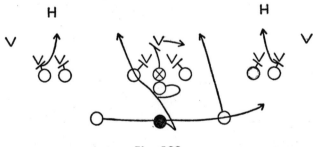

Fig. 123.

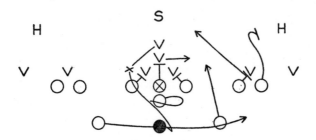

Fig. 123a. The Straight Line Defense.

faking a Hand-off and run the Counter back to the open side. The Straight Line Defense forced the offense to abandon this play. (See Figure 123.)

Although the Straight Line Defense is strong against plays directed at the center of the line, it has proved to be weak against the Option Play. Since the faking halfback can cut off the pursuing linebackers, the blockers and quarterback can put a great deal of pressure on the defensive end with the Option Play.

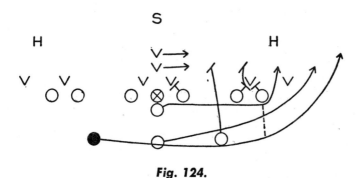

Fig. 124.

Defensive teams are frequently trying these unusual alignments, which they feel will confuse our blocking assignments, and put pressure on our splits. If they are successful, we will not move the ball well. However, as we learn more about the defense, we are able to split properly and handle any alignment they might play against our Split-T attack. The ability to understand the defensive pattern determines how quickly we can handle it. The most satisfactory planning a Split-T coach can make is to teach all of the basic offense to the best of his ability and stick with the strategy of recognizing the defense by calling the play that hits the weakness.

Offensive Problems

Most offensive problems seem to begin when some coach becomes fascinated with a new series of plays and tries to use them in conjunction with his basic Split-T. The trouble arises due to lack of time. The new plays take time away from basic attack, and not enough time is available to learn the new series well enough to depend on it entirely. Ultimately the players end up unable to run either series effectively. It seems the coaches who have dropped the Split-T when they wanted to pick up a new series of plays are wiser than those who try to mix the two attacks.

One of the most interesting groups of plays to come into the offensive planning among the high school coaches recently is the Belly Series. The Belly Series is a fine offensive attack but some of the Split-T coaches have tried to make it a part of the basic Split-T offense. The two attacks do not blend well and coaches who have tried to mix them are having trouble. The Belly

Series depends on a strong fake to the fullback. This fake is accomplished by having the quarterback place the ball in the fullback's stomach and leaving it in this position as he runs with the fullback for several steps.

To get the ball back, so that it may be placed in the fullback's stomach, the quarterback must pull away from the line of scrimmage quickly. If the quarterback moves down the line in the manner he uses on the Split-T, he is unable to ride the ball in the fullback's stomach long enough for a fake. This means that the quarterback and center must learn two methods of exchanging the ball if the team is using the Split-T and the Belly Series.

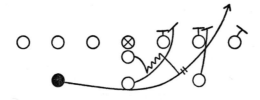

Fig. 125. The Inside Belly Play.

The Outside Belly Play blends in more smoothly with the Split-T since the operation of the quarterback is essentially the same as his operation on the Slant Play. However, a few Split-T teams who had trouble trying to perfect the operation of the Option Play have tried to substitute the Outside Belly Play as a means of running wide. This action is usually not successful, since the defense can key the maneuvers that differ radically from the Split-T. On the Outside Belly Play, the on-side half-back flares out wide to lead the blocking. Since there is no threat of a hand-off, the defensive linemen may pursue rapidly to meet the outside play.

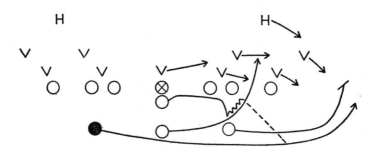

Fig. 126. The Outside Belly Play.

The teams that use the Belly Series as their major attack become so skilled in its operation that they are able to run an option, forcing the defense to respect the fake of the fullback. Their quarterback, well trained in this maneuver, will leave the ball in the possession of the fullback when the defense fails to challenge him. To become efficient in this requires a lot of practice, and the coach who tries to teach it along with the basic Split-T will have a tremendous task.

I believe the Option Play, which can be taught in less time, preserves the basic Split-T pattern of running wide. I therefore think it is a better plan for the high school Split-T coach to concentrate on teaching the basic fundamentals of the Split-T offense and not try to include portions of other attacks.

Index

M